CW00969376

The Future is Young

The world has talents:
it is time to offer them an ambition

Bruno Lanvin
Osman Sultan

The Institute for Management Development (IMD)
Chemin de Bellerive 23
P.O. Box 915
CH – 1001 Lausanne
Switzerland

Tel: +41 21 618 01 11 – Fax: +41 21 618 07 07

www.imd.org

All rights reserved. No part of this publication may be reproduced, stored in a
retrieval system, or transmitted, in any form or by any means, electronic, mechanical,
photocopying, recording or otherwise, without the prior written permission of IMD.

The right of Bruno Lanvin and Osman Sultan to be identified as authors of this work has been
asserted by them in accordance with the Copyright, Designs and Patents Act 1988.

Typeset in GT Walsheim and Adobe Caslon. GT Walsheim is a trademark of Grillitype
Foundry. Adobe Caslon is a trademark of Adobe.

ISBN 978-2-940485-55-0
eISBN 978-2-940485-56-7

About the International Institute for Management Development (IMD)

IMD is an independent academic institution with Swiss roots and global reach, founded
more than 75 years ago by business leaders for business leaders. Since its creation,
IMD has been a pioneering force in developing leaders who transform organizations and
contribute to society.

Based in Lausanne and Singapore, IMD has been ranked for more than 15 consecutive
years in the top five of the FT's Executive Education Global Ranking and #1 in the world for
open enrolment programs for nine consecutive years.

This consistency at the forefront of its industry is grounded in IMD's unique approach to
creating 'Real Learning. Real Impact'. Led by an expert and diverse faculty, IMD strives
to be the trusted learning partner of choice for ambitious individuals and organizations
worldwide. *Challenging what is and inspiring what could be.*

About the cover

The image used here attempts to illustrate the vision that the world as a whole currently
has of its own future, namely a mixture of (a) a promising dawn, (b) a darkening dusk, and
(c) a possible global conflagration. The purpose of this book is in its title: a new dawn is
ahead of us, and we can make this world better if we have enough faith in our common
future, and work hard (and together) to make it happen.

To Anne Miroux-Lanvin, my wife, for her patience, support and constructive comments during the years of work that this book required.

To my children and grandchildren Hadrien, Thomas, Victoria, Eve-Anne, Oscar, Danaé and Roméo who will be part of the generations that will define the future.

Bruno Lanvin

To Ghada, my wife, my present and hopefully and whole heartedly my future. You have always known how to highlight the good in what happens.

To Fouad, Nour, Wissam, Salim and Jade, my children. You have been my always-renewed anxiety of the future, you are today the hope and the inspiration of it. I have molded my ideas watching you become what you are today.

To Lina, Nora and Rim my granddaughters. You will always be the burning flame of youth in me.

Osman Sultan

Special thanks

The authors want to express their special thanks to Martin Kralik, who was instrumental in shaping the ideas behind this book, and producing its final version. Martin is not only an author in his own right (he recently co-authored 'Resetting Management'), but also a highly knowledgeable scholar, and a constant and eager observer and analyst of the intercultural dimensions of current trends.

Table of Contents

Preface   6

Why this book   9

Chapter 1   Do self-driving cars need
             rear-view mirrors?   17

Chapter 2   The decade's new currencies:
             data, talent, learning   49

Chapter 3   Overcoming fears   74

Chapter 4   The new landscapes, spaces and
             voices of talent innovation   92

Chapter 5   Young values are the lifeblood of the
             new geographies of talent innovation   119

Chapter 6   Revitalizing ambition and
             faith in the future   136

Conclusion   158

References   162

Figures   184

Authors' Short Bios   185

Preface

It is a privilege to be young. Our future has that privilege.

Our times are challenging ones. Previous times were as well.

Why is this century different, and why is it reasonable to think that it will usher in a new era in human history?

It is different because the problems we face have reached a new degree of urgency. Whether we consider the dramatic consequences of climate change, the likely repetition of pandemics, the constant rise of inequality, or the resurgence of geo-political tensions, we feel the need to act. And this feeling comes from our hearts and guts as much as from our brains.

This century is also different because information technologies and networks, our ability to travel to all parts of the world, have brought us the kind of planetary knowledge and experience that generations before us could only dream of.

Most strikingly, perhaps, humanity has more tools in its hands to address those challenges than ever before. We have progressively developed technologies to produce renewable energies. We have created new modes of travel and new ways of exchanging goods and services across the planet. People and ideas have been crossing borders, trading knowledge, and imagining the future together. We have expanded our capacity to express our feelings in music and other forms of art, and to disseminate them globally. Social networks have given younger generations the ability to share their observations, views and feelings in 'real time'. And within decades, space travel is expected to be an ordinary part of our lives.

Against this backdrop, I am often surprised when younger people feel pessimistic about the future. Yet, this is what we see: young 'digital natives' often spend more time on their smart phones than interacting with their neighbours, with fellow students or fellow workers. Many do not vote. Some have become allergic to hierarchies, organizations, and sometimes to science, evidence, and progress. On the other hand, I admire how many young people believe in the importance and possibility to live better lives and contribute to society based on values rather than profit. As I have from the beginning of my career, they are determined to make the world a better place.

In my life and in my work, through success and failure, I have met countless brilliant and value-driven young people. Many confirmed my deep belief that, when given a chance, everyone can grow and succeed based on their own talents. But I also drew another lesson from these encounters: those with enthusiasm and optimism have a greater chance of realizing their dreams. Every talent (however hidden or embryonic) deserves an ambition. Ambition guides talent, and enthusiasm and optimism make the ride enjoyable and creative. There are many ways to define success, but in my view two components are essential: the extent to which you have managed to make people's lives better, and the fun you've had and shared along the way.

I hope that you enjoy reading this book, because this is precisely what it is about: making the best use of your talents (whatever they may be), turning this world into a better place, while enjoying every single step of the ride (however demanding and challenging it may be).

Indeed, the future is young. Let us turn this privilege into something that our children and grandchildren will thank us for.

Sir Richard Branson
Founder, Virgin Group

Why this book

The future is now.

If ever there has been a time when future has caught up with us, it must be the 2020s.

Technology; learning; data analytics; public health: Development in all these and many other areas has accelerated to a point where people and societies feel anxious and unsure about what it will be like, ten or twenty years from now, to be human in this world.

The future is young.

Amid this fast and disorienting pace of change, many are instinctively looking to political leaders and world-renowned experts for answers. As a result, important conversations that should be going on have been conspicuous by their absence. In particular, these are conversations that should involve young people. If new paradigms are emerging that will one day govern how we live, work, learn and communicate, it is the youth that needs to be in the driver's seat of shaping them. The new generation needs to ensure that these paradigms reflect its values and priorities, as well as its outlook on the world and how it perceives its own place in the world. Young people have boundless energy, but they often lack inspiration and hope. This book is about supporting young minds' probing efforts with creative vision, energy and ambition.

The future is ours to create.

We wrote this book as an optimistic manifesto. Having explored topics that are linked to talent and the future of talent for the past several decades, we refuse to allow today's skeptical and downcast mood to turn into a self-fulfilling prophecy. We strongly believe that today's young generation – perhaps more so than any previous generation – is guided by a strongly prosocial compass and nurtures a rich set of hopes and ambitions. If these hopes are connected to a coherent vision, allowed sufficient freedom of action, and provided with the right tools, they are bound to lead us to a vibrant future that merges faith in progress with imagination and realism. To put it in one sentence: Our future is still young, and it can be shaped in any way we want it to be.

Looking forward, yet knowing where we come from

Although the ancient Greek philosopher Socrates (470 – 399 BCE) lived through a time of decline in Athenian democracy, he was undeterred in concerning himself with the pursuit of goodness. What is known until now as the Socratic method has to do with breaking a problem down into a series of questions, gradually constructing an answer. Our approach is similarly Socratic: We are conscious that starting and guiding a conversation doesn't automatically produce answers or clear-cut, definitive solutions. But it does help raise pertinent questions and frame the dialog in constructive and inclusive ways. It is our hope that the dialog will involve young people interacting face to face with national institutions, government agencies and academia, as well as employers, technology vendors, industry regulators and other organizations around the world – at community, city, region, country, and international level.

An action agenda rooted in a fact-based dialog

It has become painfully visible that many traditional frameworks and communication grids have outlived their usefulness. They have blocked rather than encouraged bringing different parts of society together for a meaningful, open-ended, no-holds-barred discussion about issues that will affect all of us. They have also been slow to accommodate the rise of new stakeholders and to reflect the realities posed by technological disruption in all segments of life. On the other hand, social networks have created an illusion of a 'global democracy' where everyone is a specialist, and noise tends to drown out signals. Fact-checking and metrics have become an essential protection against the proliferation of opinion presented as analysis, and against fake news amplified by global echo chambers.

The question of metrics – and their limits

As in all thoughtful pursuits, we need tools and handles to grasp what is unfolding around us. We also need firm departure points. We believe that the wealth of data points and trend analyses we have collected and published since 2000 in the form of a series of annual global indices – the Network Readiness Index, the Global Innovation Index and the Global Talent Competitiveness Index – are a robust volume of information and knowledge that can serve as a reliable starting point in this project. We also need to be fully aware that not all dimensions of human endeavors can be measured.

What is in this book?

The content of this book is guided by four main principles:

1. Building a prosperous future requires a deep understanding of the past and the present

2. Amid the growing velocity of change, new players are emerging. We need to capture their voices if we are to make the future a collective success

3. As we define and redefine the future, it is values and talents that will guide us in the right direction.

4. It is also organized in six chapters, each dealing with one or several aspects of the synergies and strategies required to bring our future back to where we want it to be, and to fully engage younger generations in that effort. Here is a quick summary of each of them.

Chapter 1 — Do self-driving cars need rear-view mirrors?

Looking back at our collective past (that of mankind, as well as that of our planet) is a salutary and necessary step whenever new problems arise. The past tells us that every era and every century has had its own problems. To their contemporaries, such problems often appeared insurmountable. The past also tells us that the issues faced by mankind were best addressed by those who had solutions to offer, and those who remained optimistic about the future. Considering the past before we formulate our positions on current problems also yields key lessons, including the following five: (1) At any point in time, the future is what we make of it, (2) One-dimensional thinking is a proven way to waste a crisis, (3) Our history is about pragmatic action and social transformation, (4) Technology, innovation, and talent will remain key – just like they did in the past – with a key difference: we now have more of each than any of our predecessors ever dreamed, and (5) We live in paradoxical times, in which incredible gullibility jousts global distrust: to convince, and to be convinced, we need facts and metrics. This chapter describes some of the tools that may enable us to operationalize the lessons of history.

Chapter 2 — The decade's new currencies: data, talent, learning

Data is not the new oil, it is the new air. We breathe, generate and consume data through every step we take, and every interaction we participate in. Our societies, our organizations (private and public) are undergoing accelerating processes of digital transformation, in which value is created and shared in ways that were unconceivable just a few decades ago. This often feeds opinions that regard technology as the key driver of change. This view is fundamentally flawed: never before today has the human component of our actions and strategies been more crucial, and more vital to our future. Once we acknowledge that fact, we realize how important talent and education are, and why younger generations are the key engine that will guide us closer to a humanly desirable and sustainable future.

Chapter 3 — Overcoming fears

As problems become more global, they also prove more complex, sometimes to the point of appearing intractable. Concerns about the future quickly become fears about the future. Covid has raised new fears about our collective ability to face the massive and sudden challenges of a pandemic. But, a long time before Covid struck, other types of fears had already clouded our intellectual horizons, including environmental fears, and the fear that growing inequalities would soon become unbearable. More recently, fears about a possible global armed conflict have been reignited. Fear can be a source of energy, when it triggers a wake-up call. Most of the time, however, fear is a blocking factor that freezes our brains, inhibits our energies, and obscures our judgement. Our ability to act and to address the issues of our times requires that we should first shake out our fears, and start to put all of our abilities and available tools at the service of shaping the future that we want. This includes thinking and acting on the future of work, the future of education, and possibly the future of democracy. Such efforts are all the more daunting given that we have to design them in times of growing uncertainties. We hence need to be guided by a clear set of principles and objectives. For younger generations, such principles and goals gravitate around two key notions: impact and values.

Chapter 4 — The new landscapes, spaces and voices of talent innovation

The new generations have talent, energy and values. This will enable them to change the world, and make it a better place. So what could go wrong? Well, there are many ways by which talent and energy can be misplaced, poorly organized or misguided (intentionally or not). Here again, history abounds with examples. The emergence of new ways to learn, work and interact can be very misleading in encouraging us to believe that we live experiences that no one has ever lived before. Fundamentally, the forces and mechanics at play are often very close to what they have been for centuries: survival instinct, greed, but also empathy and the will to be part of a diverse and inclusive community. Taking the example of urbanization, the concerns we face today (including in so-called 'smart cities') are much more human-centric than technology-driven.

Chapter 5 — Young values are the lifeblood of the new geographies of talent innovation

How do those younger generations define happiness? How can such a definition be combined with longer-term impact, and a value-driven society? Expression, creativity (combined, in many cultures with a romantic passion for 'disorderly conduct') need to be part of how impact will need to be defined. History tells us that time matters: a multitude of small steps do not necessarily add up to a move in the right direction, unless they are guided by longer-term goals and aspirations.

Chapter 6 — Revitalizing ambition and faith in the future

If we can ensure that the younger generations regain the faith in the future that our times require, then it is very possible that our world might be entering the age of purpose. In the transition phase ahead, empathy, sharing and caring, diversity and inclusion will be critically important. Most vital however will be our capacity to enjoy that passage. We are not there yet: to change course, we need to acknowledge today's skepticism and pessimism. Having faith in the future is the best way to make it better. We need new data – but it is a different kind of data. We need to connect history with today's young people's own impressions and experiences. Will this require a new social contract at the global level? Here too, history has a few lessons for us.

In the conclusion of this book, we try to address in a realistic but nonetheless ambitious fashion the only question that finally matters: where do we go from here? In that last chapter, we suggest a roadmap, and a few principles for successful action.

Why did we write this book?

Ultimately, this book's ambition is to influence major debates that are surrounding worldwide issues of technology, innovation, and talent. Specifically, the main objectives we have set out to achieve in writing this volume include:

- Revive the young generation's hopes and ambitions. Inspire young people to tackle global challenges in a forceful and optimistic way.

- Serve up a fact-based, well-argued value proposition about shaping the future. Anticipate and addresses the challenges we face today while reflecting deeply on and making the best of what history has taught us.

- Technology, innovation, and talent are three strong cards in our hand. Let us play them wisely as we devise an inspired game plan.

- Articulate a brief set of action messages for the various categories of stakeholders (governments, business, civil society). Organize these messages around the guiding principles we described above.

Who should read this book?

Our target audience includes the public at large (especially younger generations), government agencies (central, cities, regulators), international organizations that are committed to Sustainable Development Goals (SDGs) and are setting norms to that end, corporations and other commercial organizations, and academic institutions including business schools.

We are confident that having faith in the future is key to making it better.

We can tackle the most daunting of global challenges successfully if we give it the best we have – the best in knowledge, talent, organizing, and a youthful sense of curiosity about 'possible worlds'. In this light, what are the questions that should be on our minds today? How do we address them with wisdom and proportion? Let us outline these in the next few chapters.

Chapter 1

Do self-driving cars need rear-view mirrors?

*"...what's past is prologue;
what to come, in yours and my discharge."*

(Shakespeare, The Tempest)

Is the future knowable?

The world is bored with the future – and has been for some time. In their 1937 article 'From a Private Correspondence on Reality', literary figures Laura Riding (1901 – 1991) and Robert Graves (1895 – 1985) wrote: "The human mind has reached the end of temporal progress: the future is not what it used to be... ...The future, that is, contains nothing but scientific development. It is... ...empty of consciousness: it no longer matters."[1] Nearly 2,000 years earlier and speaking for the Stoics, Roman emperor Marcus Aurelius (121 – 180) believed that: "Tomorrow is nothing; today is too late; the good lived yesterday."[2]

As a science, future never became the darling of decisionmakers it was once expected to be, either. Graduates of future studies like to quip that "future doesn't

---

1   quoteinvestigator.com

2   Aurelius, M., 2013.

vote; neither does it pay taxes." To make things worse, the Covid crisis of 2020 showed that even when armed with computer-generated predictive models, experts struggle to forecast where current trends will lead just a few months from today.

Meanwhile, the Now has never wielded as much power and relevance as it does today. The businesses and consumers of today's digital age are just discovering the joys of real-time data. Be it with transactions, customer support, gaming, or social media, we demand instant responses and instant rewards. And we not only want it Now: For the first time in history, we can actually expect to get it Now. As societies, are we then at all interested in where we are headed, or do we simply adapt to whatever comes up? How do we imagine a future – especially a prosperous future? And is future even knowable, to any meaningful degree?...

The authors of this book are confident that it is – and that we can chart and visualize it in vivid shapes and colors.

The past: Where's that?

When trying to visualize the future, the past remains a solid starting point. It is also useful to explore the ways different civilizations have construed the past and how it relates to the future. For example, in ancient Greece, future was often foretold as prophecy, and therefore set in stone. Other traditions dreamed of a mythical Golden Age to be rediscovered and recreated. Cultures inspired by Buddhism tend to perceive life as a wheel: Missed an opportunity? Too bad – but if you're patient enough, it may well come back. By contrast, the age of Enlightenment thinks of time as travel towards progress – away from ignorance and towards peace, prosperity, and scientific discovery.

The future vs. the past: The tangled webs we find – not only in history and philosophy, but also in language

Kinyarwanda (one of the official languages of Rwanda) has three verb tenses to describe events that will take place, including one for the near future (events taking place by the end of today) and another for the far future (events taking place after today has passed). The final future verb tense is used to address the immediate future (events taking place within minutes).

The indigenous Aymara people of South America call the future qhipa pacha/timpu, meaning back or behind time, and the past nayra pacha/timpu, meaning front time. And they gesture ahead of them when remembering things past, and backward when talking about the future. The Aymara speakers see the difference between what is known and not known as paramount, and what is known is what you see in front of you, with your own eyes. The past is known, and as such it lies ahead of you. (Nayra, or 'past,' literally means eye and sight, as well as front.) The future is unknown, therefore it lies behind you, where you can't see.

The close correlation between 'what is known' and 'what you see' also applies to Indo-European languages. It is captured, for example, in the Sanskrit word veda, in the Latin video and the Czech vidět. Similarly, in ancient Greece, the original meaning of idea, derived from eidein ('to see') was 'appearance', 'shape'.

The old Romans knew that history is among life's greatest teachers (Historia magistra vitae). Contrast that with today's culture of consumerism which has just as little room – and use – for the past as it does for the future. The sociologist Zygmunt Bauman wrote in his 2007 book Liquid Times: Living in an Age of Uncertainty that our compulsive search for new sensations on the one hand is coupled with rampant forgetfulness on the other.[3] The here and now has been elevated to such a high status that yesterday's events appear irrelevant. When a public figure or a celebrity takes 24 hours (eternity in the world of social media) to respond to a tweet, that itself gets picked up as news, trending and snowballing. In these hyper-mediated times, our attention span suffers as we become glued onto a never-ending electronic spectacle, sometimes to the point of exhaustion and isolation. 'Out of touch with what is real' has become the very definition of the modern world. But without the ability to compare and to know that 'people have lived through this – and worse – before', we will constantly be trapped in the emotional upheavals and pains of the present.

The good news is that history is not just a phone book of names and dates that seem to have no bearing on our present-day reality. It is a rich and colorful tapestry that weaves together aspirations, challenges, conflict, precedents, as well as intrigue, irony, tragedy and unintended consequences. Neither do we have to search through dusty book volumes to mine history for ideas that resonate with our own experience. More and more library collections and archival documents have been digitized; some are available via content aggregators and search databases. Google Labs' NGram Viewer, for example, allows users to search for words and ideas in a database of five million books that span several centuries. During the 2020 lockdowns, a number of world-renowned museums and galleries launched cutting-edge websites and mobile apps, making more of their collections than ever before accessible remotely.

History is a source of cycles and counter-cycles,[4] of paradigms that have a way of repeating and reasserting themselves. The backdrops and the circumstances may change, but the fundamental nature of humans and societies remains remarkably stable. Granted, with every major dramatic event of the past 20

---

3   Bauman, Z., 2007.

4   Vico, G., 1725.

years we've been told: "This is unprecedented. The world has changed forever. Things will never be the same." Nonetheless, those who study history know that there are very few occurrences that cannot be compared to others in the past. And it is precisely this potential for drawing parallels between events and eras spanning centuries that endows history with its great social value.

We have a lot to learn from the past, both in terms of inspiration and practical action. For instance, just as we thought the Spanish Flu of 1918 was an obscure chapter in history, the onset of the 2020 health crisis made us reexamine the many shared issues that are underpinning both events: The germ theory of disease; the nature and characteristics of infection, incubation, and quarantine; the safety and effectiveness of vaccination; and the contributing factors such as worldwide travel and migration. Many people with no medical training have taken to reading up on the 19th-century rivalry between Louis Pasteur and Antoine Béchamp, two scientists who held widely divergent views of infectious disease. Has the world changed since their time, at all? When an idea or a particular direction in scientific research wins over another, is it on the strength of its merit, or because of marketing, sponsors, and political connections? The ambiguity is just as alive and present today as it was 150 years ago. That is why delving into stories from the past often inspires us to view our current-day dilemmas with extra depth and color.

Many centuries before Covid, air travel and industrial manufacturing, it was climate change and disease that hastened the fall of the Roman Empire.[5] Research into volcanic ash residue has led 21st-century scientists to speculate that the collapse of the Roman Republic may have been hastened by a volcanic eruption as far away from Rome as Alaska. Following Caesar's assassination in 44 BC, written records mention unseasonably cold weather, poor harvests, and food deficits.

---

5   Harper, K., 2017.

Volcanoes, vampires, and bicycles: Climate change, 1816-style

History textbooks tell us that the spring of 1815 was all about Napoleon, the looming Battle of Waterloo and the Vienna Congress that was reshaping the political face of Europe. The books never mention that at the very same time and unbeknown to western imperial and diplomatic leaders, thousands of miles away a volcano named Tambora erupted on the Indonesian island of Sumbawa. Tambora went on to propel debris into the Earth's stratosphere for another four months.

By the following year of 1816, the resulting climate disruption affected the entire northern hemisphere. Rivers and lakes were covered with ice in the middle of the summer. City streets were littered with frozen birds and other animals. The sun vanished for months on end, disrupting agriculture, striking down livestock and setting off waves of starvation and disease. A typhoid epidemic spread from Ireland to the British Isles. British troops in India were hit by an outbreak of cholera.[6]

The disruption didn't end there: With prices of grains such as oats skyrocketing amid the dwindling supply, horse-drawn carriages – then a mainstream means of transport – became unaffordable to operate. Southwest China's Yunnan province saw such a pitiful

harvest of rice for three years running, farmers decided to plant something sturdier – like poppies. Overnight, the region turned into a major producer of opium. The drug addiction that swept China over the next 20 years eventually led to the Opium Wars.

Box continued on next page

---

6   Strickland, A. 2019.

Box continued from previous page

Not all the outcomes of this 'year without a summer' were destructive, however: With most people stranded in their homes to avoid icy rains, the villa Diodati on the shores of Lake Geneva provided refuge to a gathering of artistic 20-somethings including Lord Byron, his friend John W. Polidori, writer Percy B. Shelley and his fellow author and wife-to-be Mary Godwin. When they tired of reading books, they took to penning their own stories. With the gloomy, chilly weather adding to the existing neo-Gothic, romanticized sensibility of the era, Byron wrote a poem he titled Darkness, about an apocalyptic end of the world. Mary Godwin, for her part, drafted the Gothic novel Frankenstein; or, The Modern Prometheus, today considered an early example of science fiction. Polidori, then 21 years old, put together The Vampyre, a short prose that repackaged the bloodthirsty folklore character into the aristocratic hero that inspires books and movie franchises to this day. Meanwhile, Shelley sketched out what would become a four-act lyrical drama known as Prometheus Unbound.[7]

And it wasn't just the literary types that drew inspiration from that summer's harsh climate phenomena: Scholars believe that the unusually tinged sunsets in the wake of Tambora's explosion found their way to some of English painter J. M. W. Turner's most striking canvases.

What about technology and innovation? Well, remember the horse feed that priced itself out of the market? It is believed that this is what inspired German forestry officer and inventor Karl Drais to design his Laufmaschine ('a running machine'), an all-wood, no-pedals-(yet) proto-bicycle, also known as draisine or velocipede. As clunky as this vehicle sounds, by 1817 Drais was taking it out for rides of up to seven kilometers.[8]

Box continued on next page

7   Gunderman, R. 2016.

8   Hazael, V. 2017.

Box continued from previous page

In case you're wondering why you haven't heard about Tambora before but are probably familiar with the lesser eruption of the Krakatoa volcano in 1883: We can chalk that up to the power of media as well as to scientific limitations. Unlike Tambora, Krakatoa gained a lively following in the press. And science at the time simply wasn't capable of connecting the right dots between volcanic events and climate change, thus leaving Tambora out of the spotlight until well into the 20th century.

Whatever the anxieties we face today, humankind has tackled them – and greater ones – many times before. Almost 2,500 years ago, Socrates described the youth in his home city-state of Athens thus: "The children now love luxury; they have bad manners, contempt for authority; they show disrespect for elders and love chatter in place of exercise. Children are now tyrants, not the servants of their households. They no longer rise when elders enter the room. They contradict their parents, chatter before company, gobble up dainties at the table, cross their legs, and tyrannize their teachers."[9]

Especially in crises of consciousness, the past offers startling relevance

The closing of an era, the end of an empire: Today, these themes make for dramatic headlines and punchy tweets. Few will realize that just over 100 years ago, society was gripped with the same sense of crisis. The fin de siècle - the transition from the 19th to the 20th century - was a veritable turning of the age and a time of widespread soul searching. The system started crumbling, causing untold suffering to the very people whose survival skills were invested in the system. Decades of unprecedented technological progress which brought

---

9   Patty, W.L. and Johnson, L.S., 1953.

humankind the radio, electricity, telegraph and telephone, international travel and mass production, had once guaranteed perpetual peace and prosperity. This was a time of true globalization; a time when once could travel the world without a passport; the same era that gave birth to the modern-day Olympic movement and the 1896 'Games of the I Olympiad', held once again in Athens, after an interlude of 1,500 years.

Instead, it produced a deep sense of world-weariness (Weltschmerz) and set in motion events that culminated in the horrors of the South African War (1899 – 1902; it saw history's first concentration camps), the Russo-Japanese War (1904 – 1905), and ultimately the deadly conflagration of World War I (1914 – 1918). In his book The Decline of the West, published at the end of WWI in 1918, German historian and philosopher of history Oswald Spengler (1880 – 1936) predicted that around the year 2000, the western world would enter an authoritarian era.[10] Central governments would take on extraconstitutional power, not unlike that during the demise of the Roman Republic and the rise of the Roman Empire led by Julius Caesar (100 BC – 44 BC).

Want to understand the future? Look at literature from 100 years ago

The literary talents of the late 19th and early 20th centuries continue to have an enduring appeal today, precisely because of their insight into the many paradoxes of the contemporary human condition. In their essays and fiction, authors like Robert Musil (1880 – 1942) and Witold Gombrowicz (1904 – 1969) grappled with what they saw as a crisis of rationalist, Enlightenment thinking that beset Europe in the early 20th century. Their characters struggle to connect with

Box continued on next page

---

10   Spengler, O., 1991.

Box continued from previous page

their surroundings. They dwell in an 'in-between' space where traditional values have collapsed, and new ones have yet to take hold.

Earlier, Dostoevsky's 1872 novel Demons described an outbreak of violence, arson, and murder in a provincial town whose middle-aged residents and ineffectual young liberals join an underground revolutionary movement.

More recently, in his 2013 book Capital in the Twenty-First Century, French economist Thomas Piketty brought his analysis to life through references to such literary giants as Balzac, Jane Austen and Henry James and the way capital and class structures inhabit their novels.[11]

A sense of fin de siècle returned in the 1990s, whose postmodernism gave us a similar sense of 'it's all relative'. Importantly, it introduced a plurality of voices into historical narratives – informal, oral, material histories. Are the stories of an immigrant laborer any less 'history', it asked, than the dates and names we find in encyclopedia entries, describing wars and treaties and prime ministers?

And if the transition from one century to another can prove so difficult, what about a new millennium? The run-ups to the year 1000, 1666 and many other medieval events were rife with millenarian movements which thrived on apocalyptic prophecies. Their followers firmly believed that a total transformation of the world was just around the corner. Some historians trace the militant and patriotic roots of the American Revolution to earlier millennial religious revivals such as the Great Awakening of the 1720s – 1740s.[12] 20th-century authoritarian regimes

---

11   Piketty, T., 2015.

12   britannica.com

followed a similar script, hoping for a redemption from history by destroying the world as they knew it. Communism and Nazism sought to discard the status quo and annihilate any vestiges of the past so that a new world could rise from the ashes of the old order.[13]

What are the specific lessons that history teaches us?

History is like good art: With each new generation, we gain a new perspective on it. In his own time, an artist like Picasso was not that different from 2010s' Lady Gaga: Cleverly subversive and designed to offend. Today, he is a venerated classic. Did his paintings change? No, but we have, and so have our assumptions, perceptions, and priorities.

Thus, what we consider the nature of history to be will directly shape the interpretation and conclusions we draw about the past, the present and the future – and our own place in it:

• *There is no 'one way'. The future is what we make of it*

Today's grand narratives (end of history, late capitalism, neoliberalism, commodification, triumph of the market, Uber-ization of society) often feed the view that 'the future is closed'; that there is only one inevitable path, and that path is to be pursued in a linear fashion.[14] Francis Fukuyama's 1992 book The End of History and the Last Man was once a manifesto of this worldview, arguing that with the collapse of the Soviet Union, the world had settled once and for all into liberal democracy and free-market economy.[15] Yet in reality, there is never just one way in history. And on top of that, every 'way' comes with its own price tag and to the exclusion of other paths that could have been taken.

---

13   Cohn, N., 2011.

14   Williams, C.C., 2005.

15   Fukuyama, F., 2006.

- *One-dimensional thinking is a proven way to waste a crisis*

Once we have allowed ourselves to step away from the big narratives, we find a world full of possibilities. We embrace imagination, creativity, experience, and innovation. We learn that change is rarely linear; that it is important to unlock alternative futures; to think about not only what and how things are, but also how they could be and will be. Eventually, the 'possible worlds' of new alternatives and new spaces[16] will lead us to a narrative of hope.[17]

- *History is about pragmatic action and social transformation*

Arab scholar Ibn Khaldun (1332 – 1406), often referred to as the father of the modern disciplines of historiography, sociology, and economics, pioneered a view of history as related to action; and to social transformations that succeed each other. As much as we can, we should emulate Ibn Khaldun in being historically minded. From today's standpoint, the real value of historical events, materials and artifacts is how we can connect them with our own present-day issues in any number of domains including economics, philosophy, and political science.

- *Technology, innovation, and talent will remain key – just like they did in the past*

Too often, history is sold as a TV soap opera – as tales of kings and queens, of passion, betrayal, and deceit. We must remind ourselves that, throughout history, societies made progress because of talented individuals and their quest for discovering things and making things better. Today, this paradigm remains unchanged.

---

16   Krugman, P.R., 1997.

17   Blühdorn, I., 2017.

To operationalize these lessons of history, we need tools

How to frame and grasp these new directions and apply them to the present? Unlike in the past, there are powerful tools we can use. As a matter of fact, we have more tools at our disposal than any previous generation. One of them is data. Even without designing and administering our own surveys, every year we gain access to ever heftier sets of public data which has already been collected, cleaned up and systematized for us. The volume and variety of data we can play with are impressive. Equally importantly, citing relevant data and especially quantitative measures – statistics, percentages, growth rates, forecasts… – is the lifeblood of rational debate and the best ammunition to counter emotional, extremist, and other irrational arguments.

Imagine a debate where you have drawn strong parallels from history and coupled them with relevant data points which tell a lively story of their own. For instance, it will be so much easier to start restoring young people's trust in the dynamics and outcomes of globalization if you can demonstrate:

- How many people have been lifted out of poverty in the past X years;

- How livelihoods have improved for the bottom 40% of population ('the bottom of the pyramid'[18]) across the developing world; and

- In what ways and in what measure interdependence has been a driving force for this global prosperity.[19] [20]

Data provides us with the cognitive handles we need to grasp present-day reality – especially the trends that have to do with the accelerating adoption

---

18   Prahalad, C.K., 2012

19   Friedman, T., 2005.

20   Krugman, P., 1994

of technology. Quantitative tools like rankings and indices are especially important as we live in the age of complexity where a small change in one part of the system can produce big changes in other, remote parts of the system. Due to the growing flow of international travelers, for instance – a corollary of globalization – a local development like a virus outbreak in a city in China may produce unexpected consequences on a global scale. Moreover, today's cause-and-effect relationships are rarely linear. In fact, causes are often revealed only after the fact. Multiple interactions, some invisible, tend to follow local rules and logics and therefore resist description, abstraction, and prediction. In these conditions, it is hardly a surprise that today's businesses are said to be living 'at the edge of chaos'.[21]

What about the history of technology, internet, and digital?

On the surface, the history of digital technology as we know it may appear brief and modest when compared with the hundred-year wars of the past. But let's give ourselves some credit and look at how much data, knowledge, and insight we have managed to collect and systematize during these past two decades of the new millennium.

By the year 2000, tech innovations such as mobile phones, email and commercial internet had become widespread around the world. But as the brief boom, followed by a bust, of dotcom companies showed, technological features and capabilities were much too often confused with benefits to users (just because your gadget can do something, it doesn't automatically mean that you will use that feature, let alone gain value from it); and availability of a service with business viability (it is great to capture clicks and views and mindshare, but even in the internet age, most businesses still need

---

21   Brown, S.L. and Eisenhardt, K.M., 1998.

paying customers to survive in the long haul). No one could dispute that new connectivity was in place, linking users and giving rise to new network effects and value propositions. But beyond marketing and hype, actual evidence of positive impacts on economy and society was mostly anecdotal. The stubborn gap between what technology could do (hypothetically) or promised to do and its actual contribution wasn't going away.

It was at this time that a small group of experts was formed at the World Economic Forum (WEF) with the mandate to design a framework for assessing the impact of information and communications technologies (ICT) on the development and competitiveness of nations. It was hoped that the team could propose a more evidence-based and structured approach to how public- and private-sector stakeholders should go about formulating ICT policy. The result of their effort was the Network Readiness Index (NRI; networkreadinessindex.org), first launched in 2002.

'Index' implies measuring things and collecting data. But in these early days, NRI's creators were tasked with more than that: They had to decide what indicators to include in the index – in other words, what exactly it was they were going to measure, or at least what existing metrics they could borrow from national governments, statistical offices, and other agencies. This was no mean feat – particularly considering that, at the time, the tech industry's main preoccupation was with building out infrastructure – in other words, making the networks more robust, making the internet faster.

Fundamentally, the NRI reflects and measures the way countries take advantage of the opportunities offered by information and communications technology. From the outset, the NRI identified the three key stakeholders for ICT: individuals/society, businesses, and governments, and included elements of ICT application that were novel for the time – for example, a focus on the political environment and quality of regulations. This helped frame the conversation in terms of impact and away from 'tech for the sake of tech' or 'tech in a vacuum'. Impact means development, creating jobs and producing spillover effects that benefit business, government as well as the community.[22]

The NRI has been fast to develop into an influential global benchmark for the application and utilization of ICT. Many economies utilized the NRI to design their ICT strategies, and the NRI was used and frequently quoted by leaders from the public and private sectors. Over the ensuing two decades, the NRI framework underwent one major revision, which allowed an explicit focus on the impact of ICT. Despite the challenges inherent to collecting data from more than 120 economies, the NRI chose to retain its extensive global coverage and evolved into a trusted global benchmark of the use of ICT for development and competitiveness. The focus of its most recent instalment (2019) is on making the underlying framework future-ready in the wake of new technological disruptions such as AI. In addition to issues of trust and impact that have become critical in recent years, the redesigned NRI's emphasis is on integrating people and technology with the right governance structures. This is one of the main conditions of achieving a collective prosperous future. Technological innovation is a powerful tool to reach the SDGs.

Today we can say with confidence that the NRI authors' thinking proved visionary, producing – for the first time – a coherent framework for assessing the complex and multidimensional impact of ICT on society and the development of nations. The framework's structure and inner logic not only shaped – but anticipated – many of the fundamental aspects of how we have come to plan, examine, and quantify the impact of technology on economies, governments, citizens, and societies. The authors foresaw with great clarity the extent to which technology would outgrow the hype and the mad dash of the dotcom era and become integrated with our lives over the next two decades.

---

22   Polanyi, K. and MacIver, R.M., 1944.

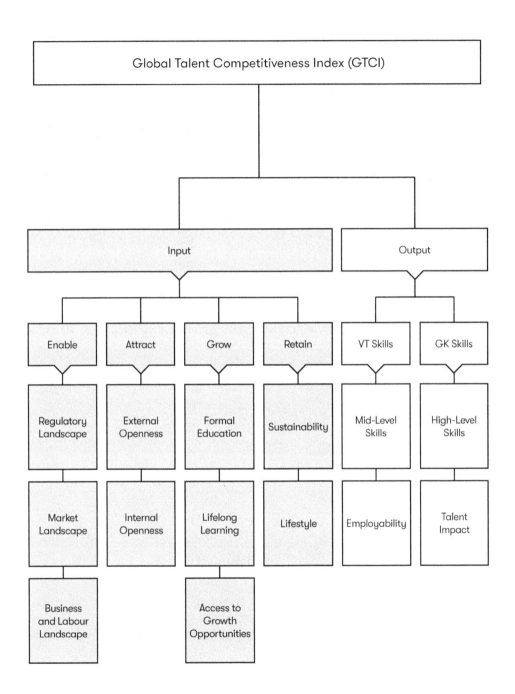

Figure 1: Global Talent Competitiveness Index (GTCI)

Meanwhile, as progress in core technologies continued at a fast pace, technology disruptions opened new opportunities for countries and companies to become more competitive through innovation. Since 2007, countries' capacity for and success in innovation has been ranked in the annual Global Innovation Index (GII; globalinnovationindex.org). Innovation, much of it tech-based innovation, is recognized as one of the main drivers of economic growth and development. In this context, GII's aim is to provide insightful data on innovation and, in turn, to assist economies in evaluating their innovation performance and making informed innovation policy considerations. Policymakers are now referring regularly to innovation and their innovation rankings as part of their economic policy strategies. Additionally, the GII is considered a yardstick for measuring innovation by the UN General Assembly, as noted in its resolution on Science, Technology and Innovation for achieving SDGs at its 74th session in 2019. At national levels, economies use the GII to design policies on innovation and intellectual property (IP). The GII report is currently co-produced by Portulans Institute and the World Intellectual Property Organization (WIPO), a specialized agency of the United Nations.

The value of an index like GII is also in showcasing the use of metrics (in many ways, 'the medium is the message' applies here as well) – and thereby encouraging economies and governments to prioritize and collect innovation metrics. Want to know where your country stands in terms of competing on innovation? Great! Then we need you to help us collect data – preferably robust, reliable, from-the-ground-up data points that can be organized into long-term, year-on-year trends and comparisons.

As issues of talent came to the fore in the global business, technology, and innovation landscapes, 2014 saw the launch of the Global Talent Competitiveness Index (GTCI; https://gtcistudy.com). The GTCI introduces the dimension of talent/human capital and its connection to competitiveness. It is an annual benchmarking report that measures and ranks countries based on their ability to grow, attract, and retain talent. It provides a wealth of data and analysis that helps decision makers develop talent strategies, overcome

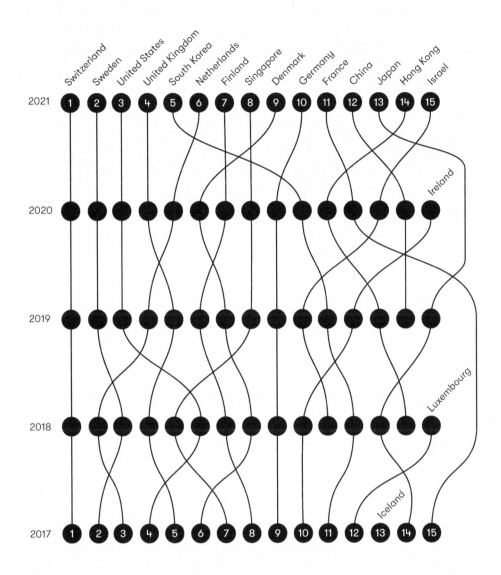

Figure 2: Movement in the GII top 15, 2017-2021

talent mismatches, and become more competitive in the global marketplace. The GTCI is the product of the joint effort with sponsors and knowledge partners from government, academia, and industry; it is an annual index created in partnership with the Adecco Group and Tata Communications.

One of the main new features in the 2020 edition is the introduction of a 'Technology adoption' component that provides a measure of how countries use and invest in new technologies, including AI. As a result, the total number of indicators has increased to 70, while the country coverage has expanded to 132. Now a regular feature of the report, the special section on cities offers a ranking of 155 cities along the various dimensions of the Global City Talent Competitiveness Index (GCTCI). With every new GCTCI edition, the focus has been on including more variables that are business- and impact-oriented – for example, those on foreign direct investment and patent applications. This is a reflection of the growing importance of the role of cities in innovation and their position as magnets for global talent.

How much have we learned in the past 20 years?

With two decades' worth of granular, worldwide data on our hands, we not only appreciate that information networks, knowledge, talent, and innovation are important. We also have a solid idea of how these originate, develop, transfer, as well as the types and measures of impact and specific benefits they create for actual communities, cities, and societies. The overall perspective, as shaped by these indices, on technology and society has evolved considerably since 2000. Unlike 20 years ago, technology's social, environmental and organizational impacts are perceived to be at least as important as its economic potential. Furthermore, technological innovation is shaping up to be a powerful instrument for achieving the UN's SDGs. At the same time, people and technology are increasingly set to interact as collaborators and partners – which opens new directions to explore, new datasets to collect, and new governance mechanisms to establish in areas such as trust, security and inclusion.

Talent as a defining theme that connects the past with the present – and the future

In the wake of the social unrest that engulfed New York in the summer of 2020, Mayor Bill de Blasio appointed urban planning expert Carl Weisbrod to oversee the city's recovery. In Weisbrod's words: "As long as New York can hold on to its talent, I have no doubt that, as an economic matter, it will recover."[23]

Once a denomination of weight in ancient Babylon, talent, from Greek talanton, originally meant 'a balance, pair of scales,' 'weight, sum of money,' and 'payment.' Only about 500 years ago did it become associated with how we think of talent today, as 'special natural ability, aptitude.'[24] For many kingdoms and fiefdoms during the Middle Ages, human presence alone was a prized commodity – especially in the aftermath of foreign invasions, civil wars and epidemics that had decimated local population. People – men, women, children – represented considerable capital. The more enlightened rulers understood that attracting settlers from elsewhere also meant bringing in new knowledge, skills, capital, and investment.

Talent wars in the XIIIth Century

In the wake of the 13th-century Tatar incursions, central and eastern Europe went through a period of what is known as Saxon colonization.[25] [26] At the invitation of Hungarian kings, German-speaking immigrants settled in sparsely populated areas, mainly in Transylvania. The term 'colonization' tends to obscure the real import of this migration wave,

Box continued on next page

---

23   Chaffin, J. 2020.

24   etymonline.com

25   britannica.com

26   theguardian.com

Box continued from previous page

which had to do with attracting talent, technology, knowledge and learning. The monarchs were keen to absorb new residents who were conversant with the German legal system; with the latest techniques of silver ore extraction and processing; and knowledgeable about advances in crafts and agriculture. The royal families were aware that these superior technologies and processes would over time be disseminated to the indigenous local populace.[27]

All transnational structures, organizations and belief systems in history have likewise recognized that. For example, when Islam reached the shores of Southeast Asia's Malay Peninsula in the 13th century, it arrived along established trade routes, on vessels operated by merchants from the Indian state of Gujarat. They brought not only a religious message but also commercial goods and advances in crafts and medicine. With the rise of early multinational conglomerates such as the East India Company (set up in 1600), the grandchildren of these Gujarati traders became trusted members of a comprador, i.e. business intermediary, class in mercantile hubs all around what some historians call the Indian Ocean Civilization – from Middle East to East Africa and Southeast Asia. Today, their descendants run IT operations in Singapore and hold professorships in Oxford and Cambridge.

As mentioned, between the 13th and 15th centuries, the use of the word 'talent' grew to mean not just money or wealth but 'gift' and 'skill'. Some historians and linguists suggest that this shift had to do with a biblical parable (Matthew 25:14–30). Reformation and the emerging Protestant ethic of frugality and early accumulation of capital – trends which Max Weber (1864 – 1920), principal founder of modern sociology, analyzed in his influential 1904 book The Protestant Ethic and the Spirit of Capitalism, may have been a factor as

---

27   novinky.cz

well.[28] Either way, talent came to be seen as not just 'what we have', but rather 'what we do with what we have.' (You will have observed that this has been one of the connecting threads that runs across all instalments of the data indices we described above – NRI, GII, and GTCI.)

Dangerous knowledge: L'Encyclopedie

The Encyclopédie is the story of one of the most revolutionary books in history, and of the young intellectuals who risked everything to write it.

In 1777 a group of young scholars produced a book that aimed to tear the world apart and rebuild it. It filled 27 volumes and contained 72,000 articles, 16,500 pages, and 17 million words. The Encyclopédie was so dangerous and subversive in its embrace of humanism and science that it was banned by the Pope and came to be seen as one of the causes of the French Revolution.[29]

The implication which has stayed with us is that talent is not meant to be locked in a vault. On the contrary, it is designed for use and for improvement that leads to prosperity. One of the factors that arguably kept the old USSR going for 70 years – through the devastation of World War II, Cold War, famines, poverty and totalitarian excess – was that its leaders understood the importance of cultivating and circulating technical talent.[30] Plucked from feudal agricultural communities in Central Asia and remote aboriginal settlements near the Arctic Circle, millions of Soviet youth received Russian-language education in the top universities and institutes of Moscow, [then] Leningrad and other metropolitan centers. Among them, women often outnumbered men. The only woman to

---

28   Weber, M. and Kalberg, S., 2013.

29   oxfordreference.com

30   Graham, L.R., 1992.

have ever flown on a solo space mission, Valentina Tereshkova (1937-), was born to a migrant family in a central Russian village, lost her father in the war at age two and before joining the space program worked as a textile factory worker.[31]

The 1990s changed everything. As socialism in eastern Europe crumbled and China and India flung the doors open to foreign investment, talent became a truly global equation. Multinationals started aggressively expanding to 'emerging markets' in Europe, Asia, Latin America, and Africa. Soon, the biggest US corporations reported, for the first time in history, earning more than 50% of their revenue from overseas rather than from their once insatiable domestic market. These tectonic shifts didn't go unnoticed. In the late 90s, a McKinsey study declared that the 'war for talent' was a critical business challenge as well as a key measure of corporate performance.[32] Similarly, the story that has emerged from the growing body of data captured in the GII and GTCI is that openness (to trade, investment, ideas, and talents) is a critical success factor in the global economy. The experiences of small but open economies (Singapore, Switzerland, and the Scandinavian nations), who had no choice but to cast the net – and their focus – wide in competing for talent and investment, bears this out with striking consistency.

Diversity as a basis for prosperity

When Ibn Khaldun arrived in Cairo, then the capital of the Mamluk sultanate, the city struck him as "metropolis of the world, garden of the universe, meeting-place of nations, ant-hill of peoples."[33]

Similarly, ancient Rome was described as a 'gathering of nations' – a veritable melting pot, in many ways as much a Greek city as a

Box continued on next page

31   Wikipedia Contributors 2019.

32   Chambers, E.G., Foulon, M., Handfield-Jones, H., Hankin, S.M. and Michaels, E.G., 1998.

33   Hourani, A., 2013 [1991].

Box continued from previous page

Latin one, and with African, Celtic, Egyptian, German and Jewish populations as well. The Roman army represented new people as well. Men from Germany, the Danube River valley or the Balkans became the backbone of the legions. Roman slaves who gained freedom could participate in society and their children were born as free citizens. Some ex-slaves became emperors' powerful advisors and common-law wives.[34] In Roman citizens' minds, one of the definitions of civilization was the willingness and ability to accept what is different.

In 2021, UNESCO inscribed the transnational property of the Frontiers of the Roman Empire – The Danube Limes (Western Segment) on its World Heritage List. Covering almost 600 kilometers (370 miles) of the Roman Empire's Danube frontier, the system formed part of the much large boundaries of the Roman Empire that encircled the Mediterranean Sea. The Roman-built structures include roads, settlements, and legionary fortresses, as well as small forts and temporary camps. They intimately related to local topography – as can still be seen today. Importantly, they served not only as a barrier but also as a bridge and a space for exchange between the Roman and non-Roman worlds.[35]

In the 21st century, talent has become a powerful magnet, a centerpiece in global business operations. Gone are the days when young graduates in many countries of the world flocked to the capital city because their hometowns had no use for university qualifications. Today, corporations are drawn to where talent can be found, particularly ample young talent. This includes not only talent that resides in developing countries, but also specifically in their tier-two and tier-three cities. As a result, during the outsourcing boom of the 2000s, multinational firms found great

---

34   Wallace-Hadrill, A., 2017.

35   UNESCO 2021.

quantities of young talent in countries such as Egypt. For its part, the Egyptian government went as far as making outsourcing skills a part of university curricula. This growing mobility of global talent has been one of GTCI's central themes. The successive rise of outsourcing, teleworking and now digital collaborative platforms has enabled businesses to source talent and innovation from anywhere in the world. It is primarily the intertwined nature of technology and talent that has been shaping the future of work (GTCI 2017).

In their 1972 book Anti-Oedipus: Capitalism and Schizophrenia, the philosopher-and-psychoanalyst duo of French authors Gilles Deleuze and Félix Guattari showed us the nomadic nature of knowledge.[36] To date, the seven editions of GTCI paint a similar picture of talent: GTCI's 2016 edition in particular focused on the international mobility of talent. Against the background of migration, it assessed the social and economic benefits of skilled talent attraction as well as the growing importance of 'brain circulation'. Few among today's businesspeople would realize that it was practically only yesterday – at the end of the 20th century – that managers and policymakers finally acknowledged talent as a crucial component in the business and prosperity equation. (Even then, it was very often reduced to 'human capital' or, worse, 'human resources'.)

What does our data tell us about talent?

In what ways has the Global Talent Competitiveness Index (GTCI) told this central story of our time? What makes countries, regions, and cities attractive to talent? And, in general terms, who has been winning the war for talent? Without getting too theoretical, the index is built as an input/output model. It looks at 1) how countries invest in developing talent; and 2) what they 'get out', i.e., the return they have realized on their investment.

------

36   Deleuze, G., 2004.

With all these data points at our fingertips, allowing government planners to measure how they are doing over time as well as when compared with other countries, especially those in the same geographic regions and income brackets, has it become easier to compete on talent? At the moment, the answer is 'yes and no.' One of the index's main findings is that talent inequalities have been going up. There are countries known as talent champions who have done well in figuring out the recipe and are pulling away from the rest of the pack. The top-ranked countries consistently include high-income economies that perform well across both the input (i.e., market landscape, education) and output (i.e. employability, talent impact) pillars of the GTCI model. On top of that, the gap between the best and the rest has continued to widen: In a twist on 'the rich are getting richer; the poor are getting poorer', it is the high performers whose competitiveness has been improving, whereas many of the lower-ranked nations have seen their talent scores stagnate.

Beyond the numbers and rankings, every edition of the GTCI has showcased inspiring case studies of countries that have consistently punched above their weight in the talent wars, and which have not only defied but overcome the odds. Moreover, the GTCI series recognized early on the importance and potential of not just nations but cities in the talent competitiveness space. Since 2017, the GTCI report includes a special section on cities and regions, and describes them as emerging in their own right as critical players in global talent. (We discuss cities and smart cities at more length in Chapter 5.)

Reshuffling the equation of talent, work, and outputs

For much of this century, talent has been the name of the game for corporations, nations and increasingly, cities and regions. It is now widely acknowledged to hold the key to economic growth and national prosperity. Just like ideas, knowledge and learning, talent is a substance that cannot be bottled up. It is shared, it grows, and opens the doors to new talent. Whatever the state of technology, talent always flows, expands, and travels the world.

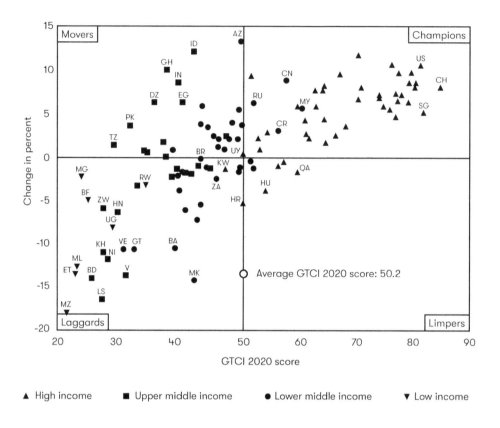

Figure 3: Talent competitiveness over time

As technology shakes up the talent scene, workers are expected to learn new things at regular intervals, absorb them and apply them to their own habits and behaviors in response to new situations and business scenarios. 'Learning how to learn' is no longer just a slogan; it is becoming the core of the majority of employment opportunities. Industry 4.0 – emphasizing data-driven processes (often running in real time), smart technology and automation – replaces mechanical process with collaboration, learning, ecosystems, and hybrid human/machine interactions.[37]

---

37   Lasi, H., Fettke, P., Kemper, H.G., Feld, T. and Hoffmann, M., 2014.

City	GCTCI Rank	GCTCI Score
San Francisco	1	76.3
Geneva	2	71.0
Boston	3	70.6
Zurich	4	70.5
Luxembourg	5	68.3
Dublin	6	67.6
Singapore	7	67.2
Seattle	8	65.8
London	9	65.5
Helsinki	10	65.6

Figure 4: GTCI 2021: Cities Index

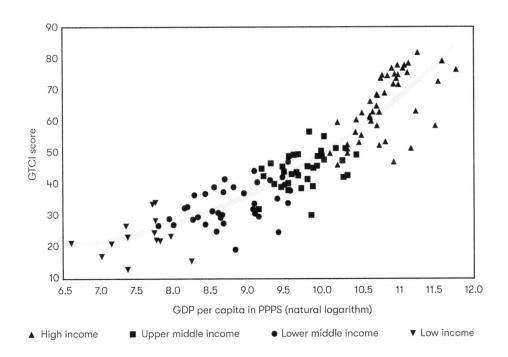

Figure 5: GTCI Scores versus GDP per capita

Against the backdrop of these dramatic changes, the inevitable question arises: Are we developing talent that employers are eager to snap up? In many countries that have gone through rapid transformation (including of the education system) in the past 20-30 years, employers have often found themselves developing their own, 'shadow' lists of skillsets they look for in a candidate. Typically, these have little to do with paper qualifications and a lot to do with natural curiosity, eagerness to solve problems, good English, confident communication, and a range of soft skills in areas like listening, empathy, and teamwork. Increasingly, the skills pyramid is a mix of knowledge, technical skills, and social competencies.

Talents are not cogs in a wheel anymore

These changes are also bringing back into focus the social, inclusive roots of learning and innovation. Talents are still required to produce business results. But at the same time, they are expected to challenge the status quo and to influence coworkers across teams. Even at the basic level, fewer and fewer tasks can be tackled by an individual. Today's employees, right across the organization, spend 50% more time collaborating than they did 20 years ago. In consequence, hiring talented individuals is not enough;[38] they have to be able to work well together with their peers, remote teammates, customers (who are increasingly involved in actual product definition and development), and even ecosystem partners from outside the company (suppliers, startups, regulators, NGOs).

History's greatest innovators rarely walked a path straight and narrow. Companies have learned that business failure is often preceded by a failure to question. For too many among the 90% of Fortune 500 corporations that have disappeared from the list since 1955,[39] the answers stopped coming because they weren't sought; management didn't look for them because they seemed

----

38   Edmondson, A.C., 2018.

39   Perry, M.J. 2019.

self-evident and well-established. Today's teams are increasingly cross-functional and cross-disciplinary, bringing together people from a diversity of backgrounds, expertise, nationalities, even personalities – including those who would have been considered 'outliers' in the go-getter, cut-and-thrust business world of just a few years ago.

Until recently, collaboration platforms including digital platforms were about stretching the innovation pipeline to include third-party suppliers and other partners. Today, it is the organization's internal boundaries that are expanding to accommodate a widely distributed workforce. For many organizations, what started as a workaround during the Covid crisis is set to open the doors to cross-location, co-creation, better productivity and ultimately, a higher level of innovation and differentiation. In tandem, a growing share of the workforce operates as 'free agents' – freelancers, short-term contractors, remote workers or digital nomads – rather than in the traditional form of salaried employment. (We will touch on the gig economy in more detail in Chapter 3.) Along the way, companies are changing their view of productivity and outputs. They are realizing that what gets done is more important than where or how.

Charting the future

In the words of Irish statesman and economist Edmund Burke (1729 – 1797), those who don't know history are doomed to repeat it. In this chapter, we have presented history as a rich source of paradigms, of which many once again resonate today. We pointed out that the logic of history is best revealed in the present, with the benefit of hindsight. 2020 has illustrated that no matter how affluent a society is, upheavals are never too far removed from the surface. Having a better understanding of how things and events past and present came about will help us prepare, take effective action and diffuse the potential for violent change.

We have also introduced the ever-expanding (in scope, breadth, and depth) body of knowledge that has become available to us in the past 20 years through cutting-edge global indices and reports such as the NRI, the GII, and the GTCI. We believe that the best way to mobilize our imagination and energy towards designing a peaceful and prosperous future is to connect the inspiration we can derive from the past with what data and evidence shows us to be productive in the present.

In the next few chapters, we will examine the action priorities for global technology, innovation, and talent. We will discuss disruptive innovation and how to overcome the fear of unrelenting change. We will talk about new challenges and new players in the technology, innovation, and talent landscape – as well as about how to empower these players and minimize their vulnerabilities. Lastly, we may not know exactly what the jobs of the future will look like. But we do know that the talented, tech-savvy millennial workforce has become a champion of human development. We need to continue studying, benchmarking, and monitoring the ways in which values and talents are becoming the bedrocks of future economy and society; and how they can revitalize, particularly among young people, faith in and ambition towards the future.

Chapter 2

The decade's new currencies: Data, talent, learning

> "Hide not your talents, they for use were made.
> What's a sundial in the shade?"
>
> Benjamin Franklin

The legend of rice on a chessboard

13th-century Arab scholar Ibn Khallikan recorded for us a parable involving a mathematical problem of exponential growth: Let's say we place one grain of rice on the first square of the chessboard, followed by two grains on the next square, four on the next, eight on the next and so on for all 64 squares, with each square carrying double the number of grains as the square before. That doesn't sound very complicated so far, does it? Except by the time we reach the last square, the total number of grains equals 18,446,744,073,709,551,615 (eighteen quintillion four hundred forty-six quadrillion, seven hundred forty-four trillion, seventy-three billion, seven hundred nine million, five hundred fifty-one thousand, six hundred and fifteen)—about 2,000 times the annual world rice production.[1] Some versions of the story end with actual heads rolling – but that's not mathematically relevant.

---

1   mathscareers.org.uk

Don't say we weren't warned – 800 years ago, no less – that this is what exponential growth looks like. Lo and behold, today we are going through the same type of acceleration in several areas of life that define our time in history. Chief among them are rapid growth in data volumes, and continual expansion in technology capabilities. In fact, some math experts believe we have been making our way through the second half of the chessboard since possibly as far back as 2006. Consumers, business, governments – we are all drowning in information and technology. Those among us who discovered the internet in its early days, in the 1990s, reminisce wistfully about the simpler times. Back then, the majority of tech-enabled products and features were brand new, exciting and full of promise. "I'm learning how to send email", our college professors would solemnly announce to class. Sharing the on-screen cursor with a friend who was thousands of miles away; reading an online newspaper from a time zone where it was already tomorrow; calling loved ones overseas through cut-rate VoIP operators – all those were baby steps for modern info-communications. But for us early adopters, reared on analog systems, they felt like a revelation.

More data was generated in the last two years than in the entire human history[2]

Fast-forward 20-plus years: Wondering 'how much has the digital universe grown?' is like asking 'how long is a piece of string?'. If we define that universe as the total volume of data we create and copy every year, the numbers have skyrocketed: According to a Global DataSphere update from International Data Corporation (IDC), more than 59 zettabytes (ZB) of data were created, captured, copied, and consumed in the world in 2020. (1 ZB = 10^{21} bytes. That's 1,000,000,000,000,000,000,000 bytes.)[3] The Covid-19 crisis gave this figure a great boost as employees switched to video communications, along with a tangible increase in the consumption of downloaded and streamed video. Another study

---

2   hostingtribunal.com

3   IDC Media Center 2020.

by IDC titled Data Age 2025 predicts that worldwide data creation will grow to 163 ZB by 2025. That's 10 times the amount of data produced in 2017. The total size of this universe more than doubles every two years. As a result, from 2010 to 2020, it is estimated to have grown about 50-fold.[4]

This explosion of data needs as much computing power as we can throw at it. That is why engineers in the 2020s aspire to reach the processing capability of the human brain for their CPUs.

This kind of growth can't go on for much longer... Can it?

In 1965, Intel co-founder Gordon Moore predicted that computing would dramatically increase in power, and decrease in relative cost, at an exponential pace. The insight, known as Moore's Law, became a self-fulfilling prophecy for the electronics industry. It also taught users to expect, nay, demand that transistors – and by extension the consumer gadgets they powered – become ever faster, smaller, and more affordable.

Since 2000, many have proclaimed the death of Moore's Law, asserting that there are natural limits to this trend and that electronics have become about as small and low-priced as they can possibly get. Laptop makers don't seek to cram infinite storage into razor-thin devices anymore, either: Instead, they rely on buyers to invest in external storage if necessary.

How important is it, anyhow, to keep up this race towards smaller, faster, cheaper? Let's bring in a few metrics: In 2020, economists at the US Bureau of Economic Analysis and the Bureau of Labor Statistics examined the tech boom that swept the American economy in the

Box continued on next page

---

4   Gantz, J. and Reinsel, D., 2011.

Box continued from previous page

late 1990s, resulting in annual GDP growth of 4.3%. According to their analysis, more than 1.4 percentage points of that growth came from efficiency improvements in the manufacturing of computers and related equipment, from investments in new computer hardware by other businesses and, to a lesser extent, from purchases of computer software. More than a third of the growth of the US economy during that period came from the tech sector. From 2007 to 2016, by contrast, the U.S. economy grew just 1.2% each year – 3.1 percentage points slower. Some of the difference can be chalked up to the 2008 financial crisis and the weak job market it left in its wake. But another full percentage point of the growth shortfall can be explained by the sharp decline in improvements as well as in new investment in IT hardware.[5]

Has the 50-year run come to an end then? Not quite. It seems that Intel and other tech giants have more tricks up their sleeve – tricks that go far beyond shrinking chips and squeezing them closer together. In the pipeline: Nanowires and stacked nanowires – packing 7,000 transistor features across the width of a human hair – coupled with new modes of layering and other packaging improvements for further density. And that's not the only direction that chip makers pursue to keep Moore's Law alive and well: There are chips with eight processing cores; interlinked servers; photonic technology that transfers data and performs calculations using light as opposed to electricity; alongside a host of other technologies.[6]

At this point, more than 5 billion consumers interact with data on a daily basis. By 2025, that number will be 6 billion, or 75% of the world's population. Every day, YouTube users upload 82.2 years' worth of videos – that's 500 hoursper

---

5   Klein, M.C. 2020.

6   Shankland, S. 2020.

minute[7] – while WhatsApp transmits 65 billion messages.[8] In 2025, each connected person will be expected to take part in one data interaction every 18 seconds. And it's not just about human users: Many of these interactions are initiated by the billions of Internet-of-Things (IoT) devices connected across the globe. Jointly, they are projected to create over 90 ZB of data in 2025.[9] According to a 2019 survey of organizations, their data volumes are growing at an average of 63% per month, with 12% of organizations reporting over 100% percent growth every month. Over 90% of participants responded that it is a challenge to make data available in a format that is useful for analytics. Meanwhile, sensors that are getting embedded into anything and everything are throwing off data that can help contextualize data. This data – along with increasing amounts of metadata (data about data) – is growing aggressively and soon will surpass all other data types.[10]

The main paradox behind today's data is that it is overabundant and scarce at the same time. Successful data analytics should deliver the right insights to the right decision makers at the right time and in the right format.[11] Its impact should be strong and clear. But in reality, meaningful data sets that accurately capture current trends and help us benchmark, predict and plan remain few are far between. Too many organizations have been seduced into believing that they can only extract valuable data from more data combined with more computing power. This 'better data = more data' school of thought has been a major contributor to the data explosion – and addiction – we are witnessing at present.

Some of you may wonder: Is there no one who can process all this data and make sense of it? Is it really that difficult? A big part of the answer has to do

---

7   Hale, J. 2019.

8   Lin, Y. 2021.

9   IDC Data Age 2025.

10   IDC Media Center 2020

11   Vollenweider, M., 2016.

with complexity. Yes, we live in an age of complexity – and that means that linear, cause-and-effect relationships that could be reliably projected into the future are becoming a relic from a different era. It also means a steadily rising number of interconnections within any given system. As a result, patterns often become visible only well after the fact.

It is within these shifting sands of deepening complexity that the global frameworks we introduced in Chapter 2 – the NRI, GII, and GTCI – are much needed to give us a grip on technology's role in the world. The metrics that are assembled in these instruments provides us with the ability to measure and examine that role across time horizons and make country-by-country comparisons. As mentioned, increasingly these bodies of knowledge also drill below the country level to study the progress made by regions and cities in adopting technology, nurturing innovation, developing talent, and building on all three of these areas to produce social and economic impact. Complexity or no complexity, policymakers and business strategists still need facts and evidence to operate and make plans, and that is what the indices provide.

Digital: Boon or bane?

Faced with the staggering pace of expansion in data volumes, the darker corners of blogsphere are lamenting the rise of 'civilization-ending technologies.' Unless we learn to deal with technology, will technology in the end deal with us? Novelist and tech writer Tim Maughan's online column, No One's Driving, regularly suggests that our world is run by vast automated systems, from supply chains to financial trading, that are too complex for any single human to comprehend – and that we are losing control of them.[12]

And this is before we introduce AI into the mix. 2021 has seen a big regulatory push towards ensuring AI systems' transparency, explainability, and

---

12   Maughan, T. 2020.

trustworthiness. Complicating these efforts is the fact that AI is reaching a level of sophistication where peeking inside the black box in the spirit of (mandated) transparency is of little use: Even developers of these systems sometimes talk about having only an intuitive grasp of the systems' workings: They refer to their own human input as 'tinkering' – i.e., largely testing different datasets, in a trial-and-error approach. In many ways, that is the point of AI capability – to outperform human workers.

Realistically – can we tame the beast of tech and data acceleration on steroids? Let's start by acknowledging that although it's on everybody's lips, digital is still a new ball game. Digital technology has been developing faster than many industries can exploit its advantages. Often organizations embark on so-called digital transformation initiatives by starting with low-hanging fruit such as embracing social media and making their products and services available online. But by tech standards, that's kids' stuff; square five or six on the chessboard. We are looking at the transformational, 2020s digital that is unfolding on squares 40 to 50 as you read this book. As such, we are just peeling off the many layers of its dynamics, outcomes and impact for businesses, governments and societies. Real transformation requires a whole new business model, and that is where companies often get stuck in the muck of execution. On top of that, studies show that for many organizations, the ROI on their Big Data initiatives turns out to be somewhere in the neighborhood of 50 cents on the dollar rather than the three or four dollars they were originally aiming for.[13]

Since 2015, the cumulative effect of digital change on businesses has been likened to a vortex – a force that pulls everything in, for the most part compels business offerings and value chains to shed their non-digital aspects, and then reshuffles the resulting digital value into disruptive business models.[14] Digital

---

13   Korzeniowski, P. 2015.

14   Bradley, J., Loucks, J., Macaulay, J., Noronha, A. and Wade, M., 2015.

entails a pervasiveness of software – and the software release process is inherently continuous and ambiguous, exerting pressure on non-digital components to adapt.[15] Additionally, digital provides but also demands immediacy through platforms such as social media. What is clear is that if we don't take the bull by the horns – by anticipating, planning, strategizing, challenging and redrawing our own assumptions – we will likely pay the price. It will either render our company obsolete – or pick it up and throw it down in a space where winner takes all, and that winner is someone else.

Disruption: The good, the bad and the ugly

Digital technologies have dramatically altered how companies deliver products and services to customers. In banking, for instance, numerous new financial technology (fintech) actors, many of them 'born digital,' have launched innovative services designed with the smartphone-addicted consumer in mind. Customers can now complete most financial transactions using their mobile devices, QR codes and other tools, which offer speed and convenience. Even traditional players with roots in the predigital era are finding that 95% of their interactions with customers take place in the app rather than in brick-and-mortar branches.

In many parts of the economy, predictability has gone out the window. So have categories like risk: To talk about risk assumes that we can predict and outline the nature of that risk. Increasingly – and as Covid-19 illustrates – that is not the case anymore, except for a few catastrophic Black Swan events. Predictability has been replaced with pervasive uncertainty. Disruption defines today's change to such an extent that companies go to great lengths to disrupt themselves.

---

15   Gothelf, J., 2014.

Self-disruption, deliberate and successful: Siam Commercial Bank

In 2016 Thailand's Siam Commercial Bank (SCB) embarked on a major digital business transformation journey in response to intensifying competition and deregulation. Seeing its traditional strengths – such as an extensive countrywide network of physical branches – turn into liabilities, SCB formulated a radical transformation plan. It included 'Going Upside Down', i.e., disrupting itself as a way to reduce costs, enter high-margin lending segments, embrace data analytics, and switch the business model to become a platform. In the process, it trained branch employees to act as relationship managers instead of processing documents.

SCB's managers understand that digital change is rarely incremental. Sophisticated data analytics allow them to target uncharted service segments such as unsecured lending. In existing segments, using design thinking and big data they devised new projects, e.g. chatbots that facilitate interaction with SMEs. They have also learned how to translate data into visual storytelling, instantly highlighting a customer's needs. For customers, the results have been a game-changer: Real-time approval, no documents required, one signature only, and access anywhere – all unimaginable just a few years ago – have become the norm.[16]

SCB can now execute at a pace to which it was not used but which is the norm in a competitive digital environment. With the main building blocks of digital transformation in place, it has set its sights on organizational restructuring to flatten hierarchies and introduce agile ways of working throughout the organization.[17]

---

16   efmdglobal.org

17   Banchongduang, S. 2021.

This is not to say that in the old days, before the proliferation of digital, running a government or operating a business were a long, placid stream: For example, in the 1980s, i.e. well before the internet and the rise of China, captains of industry routinely complained of hyper-competition. Leveraged buyouts, corporate raiders and hostile takeovers made the news on a daily basis. Every new wave of worldwide technology adoption and every industrial revolution in history have produced a pervasive, game-changing disruption that entailed social upheavals and widespread moral anxiety.

Electric lighting disrupted our millennia-old, biological clocks and rhythms of life in ways whose health ramifications we are only beginning to understand. Electricity also powered the equipment – lights, pumps, elevators – that allowed architects to build skyscrapers and make 'cities that never sleep' a reality.[18] Despite that, electricity was not unchallenged: Between 1878 and 1903, cities like Chicago witnessed a 'battle of the systems,' as intense technological competition spilled over into political conflict. As expensive electric bulbs displaced gas lighting in elite homes, gas companies penetrated working-class neighborhoods and started marketing gas energy for cooking and heating. The city hall became a battleground where gas, electric, and transit promoters vied for lucrative contracts and franchises.[19]

In its early days, the use of audiovisual equipment set off many concerns as well: By listening to the recording of a deceased person's voice or watching moving images on a screen, was society conjuring ghosts? The sense of crossing lines that had not been crossed before was all too real. Similarly, between the two world wars, radio ventured into new territories and established itself as a major political and often even religious battleground. The HBO series Carnivàle (2003 – 2005) depicts in vivid detail this Golden Age of radio in 1930s America and the social and cultural force that radio broadcasts represented. Their fictional characters entered the listeners'

---

18   AmericanHistory.SI.edu. 2019.

19   Platt, H.A. (n.d.).

worlds and captured their imaginations. For the first time, young people gained the autonomy to listen to popular music, thus spending time away from their parents and indulging their own cultural tastes and preferences. A talented orator, President Franklin D. Roosevelt (1882 – 1945) was the first American politician to recognize the radio's full potential, notably through his 'fireside chats' which gave him direct access to 30 million people, coast to coast.[20] It demonstrated the radio's hold over the listeners and the power exerted by those who mastered that medium.[21]

Were these upheavals ultimately proven to be as pervasive and game-changing as the digital revolution that is taking place at present? Only time will tell. The way we think of commercial radio or utilities like electricity and gas today probably foreshadows the way future generations will view digital: Humming in the background, non-controversial, nearly invisibly embedded into the fabric of everyday life.

Tech vs. human, tech and human, tech + human

The NRI has consistently aimed for a better balance between the technology and human dimensions of digital economy and society. Technology, people, governance and impact are the pillars that buttress the NRI model. Measuring how individuals, businesses and governments use and create impact through technology, NRI's creators emphasize the importance of the human face and values behind IT. In a post-Covid world, we will see the clock of digital transformations speed up even further. Therefore it is all the more urgent that we ask questions about to control technology and integrate it with citizens, businesses and governments. Without clarity and richness of insight on these issues, a headlong rush towards pervasive digital transformation will produce more ambiguity and unintended consequences than we know how to make sense of.

---

20   Brown, R.J., 2004.

21   Verger, J.D., 2012.

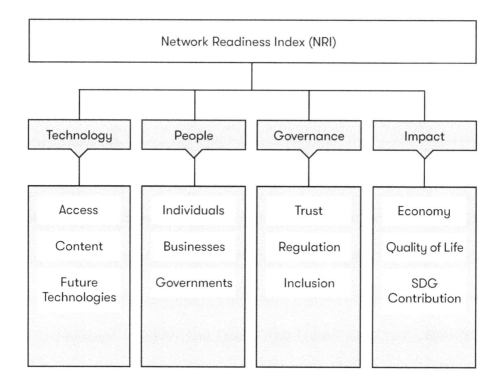

Figure 6: Network Readiness Index (NRI)

Digital transformation is difficult enough to pull off for a company. In fact, like all large-scale transformations, it is estimated that two-thirds of these change programs fail: To disrupt an organization and its people is one thing; to put the pieces back together – and steer clear of icebergs like culture, politics and hidden narratives and processes (there we have it; once again, the human aspects) – is quite another. And if the odds of winning are one in three for a well-oiled corporate machine, armed with trainers, coaches and consultants, where does that leave societies? Can a country's core be digitally transformed? Can countries afford to run the risk of failure in undertaking that transformation?

Digital is now one of the main avenues that lead us towards fulfilling the UN's SDGs, rebuilding global cooperation and redefining globalization. Citizens are told that "technology is set to transform the everyday life of billions." Many are confused because they've heard it before. Ever since the first mobile phones came out, tech vendors have been selling that vision. Around 2005, many tech programs specifically targeted the 'bottom of the pyramid', i.e. the largest but poorest consumer segments in places like South Asia and Africa. In hindsight, providers often confused digital initiatives with digital strategies, and technological features with actual value-adds. Even in developed, affluent markets, day-to-day life in the 2020s continues to resemble The Brady Bunch or Friends much more than Star Trek.

As the NRI has outlined, citizens, corporations large and small, and central as well as local governments will only be comfortable with digital tools and environments if they can enjoy safeguards in the following areas:

- **Trust:** How safe individuals and firms are in the context of the network economy.[22] This does not only relate to crime and security but also to perceptions of safety and privacy. How trusting is the environment; how trusting are the prevalent behaviors.

- **Regulation:** The extent to which the government promotes participation in the network economy through regulation.

- **Inclusion:** The digital divides within countries where governance can address issues such as inequality based on gender, disabilities, and socioeconomic status.

These are the governance frameworks that must be in place if societies are to anticipate and shape the impact of emerging technologies. Their absence would create scenarios where the digital revolution, like all revolutions, eventually devours its own children. The realization has emerged that if we are not able to leverage technology for bringing out the best in humans, we are

---

22   Chakravorti, B. and Chaturvedi, R.S., 2017.

potentially headed for scenarios in which society is fractured and some of our core organizational principles, such as democracy, can be perverted. The old saying, 'a democracy typically chooses a free market, but a free market doesn't necessarily choose democracy' is equally applicable to the interaction between democracy and technology.

From open to data-driven: A new geography of innovation

Open innovation has been with us for many years. In the early 2000s, many multinational companies had it thrust upon them through a rude awakening: As if out of nowhere, an unknown startup would emerge in China and 'blow their business out of the water' (and oft-heard phrase at the time) by offering customers a comparable, better-priced, and in some cases superior product. That's when the realization dawned on companies that to innovate competitively, they could no longer go it alone and pursue product-improving experiments behind locked doors. Keeping the cards close to one's chest was not practicable anymore. At that point, corporations threw their R&D and innovation pipelines open to partners around the world – academic institutes, R&D centers, science parks and technology hubs as well as incubators, accelerators, and new tech ventures. They also started joining and setting up innovation clusters that typically brought together, in one physical location, a private-sector vendor, a government or academic research institute and a university. This gave them access to yet-to-be-commercialized research and technology in addition to a pool of young talent. Some clusters and the pools of investment, facilities and talent they accumulated became robust to a degree where they could start marketing entire regions within countries as innovation movers and shakers (e.g., Flanders). Other consolidated with peer clusters to establish a national innovation system (Namibia).

For a number of years, the GII has kept track of the innovation story and how it earned a central place in corporate strategy as well as national economic growth strategies. It identified and captured many new and promising trends toward democratizing innovation beyond a select number of top economies and clusters only. For example, by 2018, research and development (R&D) spending grew by 5.2% a year, i.e., significantly faster than global GDP growth.

In the past decade, digital has reshaped the nature of innovation processes. It has channeled innovation into a number of new directions. In keeping with the dynamics of the digital vortex, innovation focus has shifted away from R&D as an avenue that leads towards new materials and products. Instead, the action is in new business models, new delivery channels and new ways of creating and capturing value. These processes have blurred the dividing lines among companies and industries, bringing analysts' attention to networks, ecosystems and value arenas. In the past, an ecosystem might include a company's suppliers and other partners, largely from within the same industry. Today, thanks to digital, companies like Starbucks, Ford and Amazon can join forces in one ecosystem. Coursing through that system as its lifeblood is data which allows customers who drive a Ford vehicle to order their Starbucks coffee through Amazon's Alexa voice service.[23] But the impact of shared data doesn't stop at convenience: It also allows this diverse assemblage of companies to observe and learn from user segments and spending propensities in other industries, which historically they had little interaction with. The result: Win-win and learning outcomes all around the ecosystem.

In recent years, data-driven innovation has revitalized older marketing concepts such as the long tail of distribution.[24] Overcoming the constraints of inefficient distribution and greatly improving supply-and-demand matching, companies like Netflix are able to personalize their offers and essentially consider every customer to be a 'segment of one.'

---

23   Soper, T. 2017.

24   Brynjolfsson, E., Hu, Y.J. and Smith, M.D., 2006.

Netflix: Treating every customer as a 'market of one'

Netflix has become an expert on what media content within its global library viewers prefer, how to optimize its recommendation engines for them, and what type of marketing they respond to. Using technology, it has reconceived viewers' end-to-end experience[25] and essentially treated every customer like a market of one. Thinking beyond country markets and business lines, Netflix has successfully and systematically infused a sense of direction and community into a global market.

Data *alone*, when sliced and diced digitally and imaginatively, opens up endless possibilities for innovation

More and more commonly, it is insights from real, live data – rather than historical data, third-party surveys and other market research projects – that directly inform planning and decision making. Encouragingly, this doesn't occur only at digital-native operations such as Amazon or Netflix: For instance, at companies like Nike, an AI-run mobile dashboard feeds management sales performance data by outlet, on an hourly basis.[26] Integrating and questioning that data, finding meaningful patterns and translating those into insights is bound to bring decision making and strategizing to a qualitatively new level.

Likewise in public domains, the potential that is associated with collecting and aggregating live data is mind-boggling: Imagine an intelligent transportation system that is enriched with a machine learning framework:[27] Live, granular

25   boardmember.com

26   Mixson, E. 2020.

27   Mena-Yedra, R., Gavaldà, R. and Casas, J., 2017.

traffic information is shared and predicted in real time by all vehicles on the road. The result? The old traffic rules – general, hypothetical and presumptive – are not needed anymore. The traffic itself is the rules. Drivers respond to what is in front of them, not what could be, might be, or used to be. That is the power of complex adaptive models – something we will see more and more of in the next decade.

In the past, obstacles standing in the way of data analytics projects often included a lack of necessary data granularity.[28] Today, companies are also learning how to go through data with a fine-comb view, separating the wheat from the chaff – the chaff being commodified, undifferentiated offerings that don't add value. In a number of industries, this fine-grained combing is known as de-averaging, i.e. replacing historical and hypothetical patterns with live data aggregates. Traditional businesses love to look at averages such as sales by country, by category etc. But what do the averages actually tell us about real customers and emerging trends? Not much – by definition, they obscure rather than elicit all that exciting information and insight. The resulting broad-brush approach results in budget misallocations and unidentified – or simply unserved – growth opportunities. How to escape the trap of averages? By collecting, continually and consistently, lots of real data from business lines, countries and product categories. That pool of near-real-time, frequently updated data can then be mined for patterns including predictions. A keenly analytical, granular view will bring into sharp relief what is viable and what isn't.

These practices in data-driven innovation show that innovation doesn't die when we run out of ever more complex devices to design. Often what we need to examine is how to optimize the use of our existing capabilities and explore new architectures of knowledge. There is never just 'one way'; every approach we take comes with the exclusion of other, possibly superior or more flexible approaches.

---

28   Sargent, J. 2019.

Organizational innovation is one such example of redesigning 'what we have'

For the past 100 years, frontline, customer-facing staff were at the bottom of the food chain in most companies, physically removed from senior management by many layers of hierarchy and bureaucracy. Today, customer-centricity is the mantra and has been recognized as the source of much competitiveness. The frontline is 'where it's at', to such an extent that power is progressively shifting down the chain. Not only that – companies are aggressively flattening their organizational structures, releasing great internal flexibility and resilience in the process. Among radical organizational innovators such as China's appliance maker Haier, the frontline is only 1.5 or two layers of admin away from the C-suite. In some consumer segments, such as retail banking, involving the customer or end user early, closely and hands-on in the actual product development means that many processes can be simplified from 20 steps to three.

Organizational innovation at Haier: From state-owned enterprise to a network of microenterprises

China's global appliance-maker Haier, once a creaky state-owned entity (think 'all about quantity, not quality; and keeping people on the payroll to keep the government quiet') has actively disrupted and flattened itself to a point where there are just 1.5 hierarchical layers left between the C-suite and the frontline. It runs as an open, dynamic marketplace of thousands of self-organizing teams governed by a few simple rules ('the Haier constitution'). The entire organization has become a wide network of empowered entrepreneurs, tapping extensively into an external source of ideas and business acumen from end users, suppliers, road show participants and other partners.[29]

---

29   Zhang, R. 2018.

Can talent keep up with all this acceleration?

Just as data is the currency of digital transformation, talent has established itself as the new currency of the entire global economy. Even the most tech-oriented among corporate and government leaders will readily acknowledge that it's not companies that transform; it's the people. For digital change to take root, they are the ones who have to change their behaviors and habits, pick up new skills, and develop new mindsets.

According to the findings published in the GTCI, the human factor is the most important resource for national economies to improve their competitiveness and innovativeness in a sustainable way. The main issue facing talent and talent planning is that whereas the rates of technological evolution and innovation are rapidly accelerating, talent is not a short-term trend that can change course at will. Addressing the mismatches between demand for and supply of skills, at both national and regional, especially city levels, has been one of GTCI's recurring themes.

The trends that are captured in GTCI – such as the talent gap between high-income nations and other countries widening rather than shrinking – call for embedding flexibility and resilience in talent landscapes. The technological and organizational changes we described above have redrawn the space where talent is developed and deployed. 'Climbing the career ladder' is turning into an outdated paradigm in companies that have abandoned or modernized their old hierarchies and top-down, command-and-control management systems.

Does that mean that young people are facing universally bleak employment prospects? Far from it. What it means is that the talents and skills that will stand them in good stead in their full-time jobs will likely come from areas like teamwork including remote and/or online collaboration, communication, verbalizing and visually representing ideas, influencing others, honing a sense of empathy and compassion for customers. (In the customer-centric enterprise, empathy and compassion are treated as competences, not just 'feelings'.[30])

-----

30   Frost, P.J., 1999.

Job rewards and incentives – not long ago a major sticky point in organizational renewal (with many companies encouraging their people to refocus on A but continuing to reward them for B) – are now overwhelmingly skewed towards contribution to teamwork, developing others and organizational learning. The distributed leadership that permeates the new, lean, agile organizations demands that rank-and-file employees exercise leadership as well. Unlike in the past, organizational learning increasingly draws on insights derived by junior managers who get out of the office to map out stakeholder pain points, consult non-traditional sources, uncover patterns and are unafraid to revise their own assumptions. The resulting learning and sharing of ideas with peers are some of the cultural pillars in innovative organizations.

There's no getting away from STEM subjects

Coming back to digital and data, it is worth reminding ourselves that among companies that have transformed into, for example, agile processes and methodologies, up to 70% of 80% of their product development teams is composed of data analysts, IT workers and software programmers. Along with mathematics and statistics, these are skills that will be in demand for many years to come. This accounts for the many national debates surrounding STEM (science, technology, engineering, mathematics) and the emphasis placed on STEM in education curricula. Malaysia, whose national school system largely abandoned the English language in the early 1970s, has been experimenting with not only teaching more STEM subjects in public schools but teaching them in English. Meanwhile, educators across eastern Europe are discovering that local STEM-focused secondary school graduates are extra likely to pursue their university studies abroad. As talent currencies go, STEM is clearly in a league of its own.

L. (25), Software Engineer, Redmond, WA
From rural Slovakia to Microsoft headquarters

What was the learning trajectory of a local uni graduate who landed a full-time job with a global tech giant?

- L.'s parents never went to college and therefore could only provide limited guidance.

- In high school, L. was a gifted math student. But while his peers in big cities and other countries were busy learning how to program in Java and C+, his school offered no programming courses.

- On a field trip, L. learned that math skills were a good foundation for college programs in IT, whereas coding could be learned more or less from scratch. Nonetheless, he stuck to math in his university studies.

- He never considered applying overseas – to highly ranked schools in the UK, US, Germany, or Switzerland: The prospect seemed partly too costly, partly intimidating. His advice to fresh high-school graduates: Don't be deterred by high fees or other obstacles. If you can 'get in', you will find a way to stay. Big-name schools don't necessarily impart more knowledge or skills, but their reputation goes a long way in the job market.

- In hindsight, it was the emphasis on theory and algorithms rather than specific technologies (most of which will become obsolete within 5-10 years), as well as on fast and efficient learning through analyses and proofs, that turned out to be the strong learning foundation that eventually opened doors in the global job market.

- In addition, L. feels that the skills he acquired in analytical and critical thinking have served him well in reflecting on social and political issues.

Source: Denník N (dennikn.sk)

Temporary and flexible work are also avenues to employability

Findings by both GTCI and OECD's PISA Test also point to the value of temporary work and flexible job assignments. Young people who combine full-time education with part-time employment do better than their peers in school-to-work transitions. They report lower likelihoods of being unemployed or NEET (not in education, employment or training),[31] higher wages, greater chances of pursuing apprenticeships and traineeships, and greater satisfaction with their career progression. For instance, call center positions are often maligned as high-pressure, low-wage jobs. What their critics overlook is the opportunities call centers provide in terms of training, self-awareness, the ability to rise quickly through the ranks and supervise others, including remotely, and therefore team leadership.

Much has been written about the gig economy of temporary, occasional or other nonstandard work. Estimates show that about a third of US workers take part in it, and an equal share of companies hire gig workers extensively.[32] How short-term work arrangements have solidified into an entire sector of national economies, drawing in millions of workers and creating a trillion dollars' worth of output, has a lot to do with technology: It was mostly digital, and especially digital apps, that have lowered barriers to entry so much that 'gigs' have become easily accessible to an unprecedented number of people.

By its very nature, the boundaries and precise definitions of the gig economy have been tough to establish reliably. When hearing the word 'gig', some people immediately think of Uber, the e-hailing and ride-sharing service. It is true that in large metropolitan centers, thousands of people including students,

---

31   data.oecd.org, ilo.org

32   Duszyński, M. 2019.

young graduates and even young professionals are plying the city routes as Uber drivers, trying to earn or supplement their income. But there are dozens of other gig worker categories – on-call, part-time, contingent and other workers – about whose motivations and fortunes the world knows very little. And know more it should: There is a huge difference between accepting gig work voluntarily (in some cases virtually with no pay – just like in full-time employment, for many workers money is not the only motivator; it may not even be the primary motivator) and taking the plunge because of economic hardship and because they see no alternatives; whether they maintain a full-time job alongside their gigs; and whether the gig work is their primary source of income or just a source of extra cash.

Importantly, are the gigs a virtue out of necessity? Given the chance of a regular – or better – monthly paycheck, how likely are gig workers to abandon or deprioritize their part-time work? In a survey by PYMNTS, 76% of gig workers reported that they would not quit their gigs for a 'real job'.[33] That is a counterintuitive finding, given that not being a part of the conventional workforce largely disqualifies them from applying for house mortgages, car loans and many other financial services. Are gigs here to stay permanently, and possibly continue growing? Clearly, to have a better grasp of future trends in work, digital, youth employment and urban life in general, we need to observe and learn about this phenomenon a great deal more. In 2001 – well before the days of smartphones and Uber apps – activist Barbara Ehrenreich caused a stir with her book Nickel and Dimed: On (Not) Getting By in America. In the book, she documented her three-month experience as a minimum-wage earner working in a restaurant, Wal-Mart, hotel, nursing home, and elsewhere.[34] 20 years later, a gigs-themed refresh of her work, complete with socioeconomic and political observations and predictions, and ideally with a healthy set of metrics, may be long overdue.

---

33   securecdn.pymnts.com

34   Ehrenreich, B., 2010.

H. (29), Grab driver, Kuala Lumpur, Malaysia

H. came to the capital city 10 years ago to pursue his studies. He is an engineering graduate who was laid off from his first full-time job with a local civil engineering company. He is single and shares a modest rental flat with two friends. H. doesn't splurge and rarely goes out. Still, the cost of living in the big city has gone up dramatically in the past few years. To make ends meet, on most weekdays H. borrows a relative's second car and works as a driver for Grab, Southeast Asia's version of Uber. Once his daily earnings reach RM100 (about US$24), H. sends the car back to its owner's house, gives the interior a thorough clean and returns home. In the evenings, he sometimes dabbles in online forex trading and has invested in Bitcoin.

The Grab gig has allowed H. to interact daily with people of all sorts of nationalities and backgrounds. His spoken English has improved considerably. But when asked if he would one day like to put his engineering knowledge and skills to use again and apply for a permanent position that comes with prospects of career advancement, H. says he hasn't thought about it. At present, he receives cash payments from Grab every day and he enjoys the flexibility of being a master of his own time.

Source: Denník N (dennikn.sk)

Are we future-ready?

Entering the 2020s, we continue moving ahead on the chessboard of exponential growth in data and in technological capabilities. Our ability to bring together technology, innovation, and talent in ways that are mutually reinforcing is what it takes to earn the label of 'future-ready'. To be considered prepared to face the economic, technological, and social challenges of the future, we must continually ask ourselves, our schools, businesses, and government agencies:

- Is the talent we produce compatible with data-driven organizational cultures, data analytics, AI-human algorithms, and collaborations? Does it reflect the desired mix of knowledge, technical skills, and social competences?

- Are we collecting the right metrics – at national, regional, and city levels? Particularly about new, emerging talent demographics and categories of workers?

- Does the statistical data we collect reflect the new, post-Covid practices in education and employment?

The 'tech + innovation + talent' equation is evolving so fast, the definition of 'future-ready' already looks different than it did a few years ago. This change is part of the new normal; its pace will not diminish. But it is not linear change, and neither is it easy to grasp and direct. In the next two chapters, we look at what this means for education, and we trace the rise of new types of players in the geography of future-readiness.

Chapter 3

Overcoming fears

"Ignorance is the parent of fear."

Herman Melville

Amid Covid, a new nature of change

Much has been written about the 2020s as a series of fundamental resets. The truth is that with or without the Covid health crisis, big resets – economic, social, political, cultural – have been a long time coming. Let's look at the titles of the winning case studies at the 2019 EFMD Excellence in Practice awards: 'Accelerating digital transformation at…'; 'Accelerating leadership transformation…'; 'Accelerating leadership insight'… Great, momentous changes have been afoot for years now, and embracing them requires that businesses, societies and governments act with decisiveness and agility.

The health crisis of 2020 hasn't pushed us into wholly unknown territory or practices that had been unheard of. In fact, very few of the trends that 2020 ushered in are actually brand new – as radical and disruptive as they may seem: We've all worked from home, telecommuted and videoconferenced for as long as the internet has been with us. We did so occasionally, as an exception and aberration to an otherwise unyielding paradigm of what work, and life, were about. The events that started in 2020 didn't thrust these upheavals in our laps. What they did was burst the dam of pent-up but suppressed change that had been swelling for decades.

That old paradigm was about bureaucracy, hierarchy and control. It was 'scientific' by the standards of 19th-century scientism. It is quite remarkable how long it stuck around. Since WWII, scholars of management as well as inspired leaders have sensed and actively suggested that there must be a better way. But for as long as the command-and-control, assembly-line style of doing things was predictable and profitable, their ideas remained confined to theoretical journals.

What 2020 has produced is more akin to a marked acceleration of existing trends. Even more importantly, it has forced us to do what we singularly avoid doing – i.e., hold up our (unspoken and therefore forgotten) most fundamental assumptions to the light and re-examine them. What is our definition of work, output, productivity? Has digital reshaped them or just added an extra dimension to them? Where do people fit in with all this? And if we believe the workforce is changing, shouldn't education anticipate and reflect these changes?

The second death of distance

Remember when physical, geographic distance died, the first time? The early days of the internet brought so much excitement about the digital world and its virtual geography that many observers predicted the death of cities.[1] Others foresaw a business world of instant, spontaneous, one-off supply chains: A factory in Kazakhstan is quoting good rates this week – click! All these wild expectations illustrated the internet's elusive, seemingly non-physical quality. We knew what it was (computers connected with phone lines), but where it was – that question has never been fully answered. Is it a network, a service, or a utility like any other?... While our understanding slowly solidified, we saw many governments and property developers aggressively invest in cyber-ports and internet parks, serving up a fusion of the virtual with the physical. As of the early 2020s, the debate continues.

---

1   Kolko, J., 2000

The Covid travel restrictions shrank the world geography further and made virtual communications – meetings, reunions, elections – the big winner. During the lockdowns of early 2020, a number of world-renowned museums and galleries launched cutting-edge websites and mobile apps, making more of their collections than ever before accessible remotely. But it isn't just physical distance that continues shrinking. Around the world, organizations took a hammer to hierarchical distance, cultural distance, power distance. When Thomas Friedman's book The World is Flat came out in 2005, few 'flat-ists' could have imagined just how flat the world and its institutions would become just a decade and a half later. Since the dawn of the information age, scholars and managers alike sensed that the worlds of possibilities ushered in by digital technologies would never sit well with the old-school, factory-production systems it inherited. A 1994 book by Elizabeth and Gifford Pinchot boldly proclaimed The End of Bureaucracy [and the Rise of the Intelligent Organization].[2] 24 years later, a front-page story by the Harvard Business Review did the same – and managers around the world were every bit as surprised.[3]

It goes to show that throughout history, bureaucracy has been a tough beast to tame, and much smarter than anyone expected: After all, if there ever was one thing at which bureaucracies exceled, it was pursuing and clinging to power. Ostensibly set up to support and facilitate other parts of the enterprise – essentially, to keep things moving – bureaucracies and bureaucrats never failed to take over and dictate. If nothing else, they were champions at clogging up managers' bandwidth with endless requests, keeping their focus and attention away from 'secondary' things like customers and sales targets. A 2014 study by Bain & Co. revealed that in a single large company, supporting and running the weekly executive committee meeting devoured 300,000 man-hours a year.[4]

---

2   Pinchot, G. and Pinchot, E., 1994.

3   Hamel, G. and Zanini, M., 2018.

4   Mankins, M., 2014.

By the time the 2020s arrived, globalization, digital and the pervasive volatility and unpredictability of the external environment had shattered any remaining illusions about the value of bureaucracy and hierarchy as dominant structures. Nearly all businesses saw their competitive advantages come under pressure – from startups, deregulation, China, and a host of other factors. Digital platforms have blurred and dissolved industry and, increasingly, company boundaries, replacing them with ecosystems, collaborative partnerships, and open innovation. Once unshakable categories like best practices are becoming a poor fit for the pervasive uncertainty that reigns 'out there' and giving way to next practices. To put it simply, the old world that could be run through rulebooks, paperwork, and ritualized meetings doesn't exist anymore.

Unlike before, in the 2020s the end of bureaucracy is not just about theoretical models. This time, business leaders are shouting it from the rooftops. And the change they have created is far from academic: Across industries, companies are transforming into networks of small cross-functional and cross-hierarchical teams which invariably include digital talents. These teams liaise with consumers, authorities, retailers, distributors, suppliers, and other stakeholders to learn and continuously adapt their organization's response.

The world can't get rid of distance fast enough

This was the context in which Covid struck: Businesses, institutions, and organizations in general eagerly dismantling distance. To survive and remain competitive means that customer-centricity rules. (True, we talked about 'customer intimacy' and 'customer pain points' etc. a good 20 years ago.) If we allow layer upon layer and silo upon silo to separate us from the customer, in this digital age, we're as good as gone. During the first wave of the health crisis in the spring of 2020, to ensure business continuity some companies went as far as 'short-circuiting' internal bureaucracy and in many cases even country managers' standing as the king of the hierarchy. For the majority of companies, the primary mission was to protect the health and safety of clients and employees, implement home office, keep morale high among employees, preserve the top line and preserve cash. This was no time for drawn-out restructuring exercises or for wringing new initiatives through committees and waiting for their approval.[5]

Most meetings moved online – but that wasn't the main shift. The entire meeting culture jumped onto a new plane: Managers soon realized they needed a shorter, more decisive and continuous approach to meetings. Define the problem. Discuss. Make a decision. Communicate it, on the spot, to the rest of the company so that employees have a sense of direction and a degree of stability in the midst of the soul-crushing news headlines and other uncertainty.

What is it we are taking apart and putting back together?

Many imaginary holy animals have been slaughtered since the beginning of 2020. Most of them were mental constructs we were clinging to for the past hundred years or more, regardless of whether they were still useful and relevant to the changing world around us. Realistically, however, will all bureaucracy be ruthlessly cast aside? Unlikely. Reinvented, perhaps. Modernized and transformed, definitely. Will the measures that companies introduced overnight last forever? Again, that's not necessarily how things work. To remain relevant, businesses will still have to respect the complexity of their global presence. That means pushing through global initiatives but also respecting local variations and preferences. Many decisions will take time to mature.

For decades, companies have been opening up their R&D and innovation pipelines to attract external partners. A similar expansion in boundaries and horizons has now turned inward: During the 2020 lockdowns, some

---

5   Girod, S.J. and Králik, M. 2021.

businesses used digital communication and collaboration platforms to come up with new customer offerings, sometimes within very short timeframes of 24-48 hours. This was a great showcase of how to speed up innovation as well as execution by drawing on the collective knowledge and experience of various stakeholders. Today, it is organizations' internal limits that are stretching to accommodate a widely distributed workforce. Digital collaborative platforms have become powerful tools for accommodating as well as motivating that workforce. In addition, using these tools amplifies the social and inclusive nature of innovation and co-creation.

New ways of thinking, learning, and knowing

Adult learning is said to work best on a self-directed basis: Adult workers look for information as and when they need it to complete their work tasks. In contrast, 75% of information that isn't applied in the real world will be lost within days; scholars call it the forgetting curve.[6] With support and encouragement from the employer, self-directed learners can become established as thought leaders. At a growing number of international corporations, staff are known to publish research papers and present at conferences and other industry events. Thought leaders are naturally attracted to peer learning and teaching. These also help employees learn how to listen to others and challenge their colleagues in a constructive way. In the words of Lebanese philosopher and diplomat Charles Malik (1906 – 1987): What you know, or think you know, that you cannot articulate in such a way as to share it with all mankind is not knowledge. It could be faith, it could be feeling, it could be intuition, it could be hallucination, it could be daydreaming, but it is not knowledge. It remains your private property until you manage to convert it into knowledge, namely, until you succeed in communicating it to others, indeed potentially to all mankind. Knowledge is essentially publishable and shareable.

---

6   Glaveski, S., 2019.

Systems thinking, data-driven decision making

Making linkages between the inner world and the external reality is also referred to as systems thinking.[7] Modern-day organizational scholars are increasingly borrowing concepts and theories from natural systems (weather patterns, biological populations) and applying them to organizational systems. They have suggested that much of what today's businesses are trying to figure out has to do with the challenge of operating as complex adaptive organisms.

Systems thinking at Toyota

As novel or theoretical as the concept may sound, it was systems thinking par excellence that gave birth to Toyota as an automobile manufacturer as well as its culture of continuous quality improvement. In the 1930s, Eiji Toyoda's cousin Kiichiro decided to expand the car engine business, which had been just an offshoot of the family's established textile loom company, into a standalone unit. Collectively, this team instilled in the Toyota workforce the culture of looking from the outside in, adopting a competitor's perspective and actively searching for weak spots that could be strengthened through better processes.[8]

The Toyota management culture under Eiji's leadership was about much more than 'lean'. Eiji was raised in his father's textile mill, which gave him exposure to machines and business. For the rest of his life, he retained a unique ability to spot and minimize waste.[9] Rather than assign factory staff – managers, engineers, assembly-line workers – their places as replaceable cogs in the machine, the Toyota system was rooted in and designed along the workers' individual as well as

Box continued on next page

---

7   Weinberg, G.M., 1975.

8   Cossin, D. and Hwee, O.B., 2016.

9   Tabuchi, H. 2013.

Box continued from previous page

group powers of observation, critical judgment and natural inclination to improve and enhance the end result of their effort. In a message to Toyota managers, Eiji wrote: "I want you to use your own heads. And I want you actively to train your people on how to think for themselves."[10]

There has been so much more to embracing digital than working from home and moving meetings online. Today's business leaders are building data-driven organizational cultures to make informed decisions based on facts. Building up a data culture means that leaders understand, appreciate, decide, and act on data much of the time, instead of rank, routine, precedents, or anecdotal evidence. Increasingly, these data cultures will replace hierarchical, relationship-based ('old boy networks') and ego-driven organizational cultures. As such, there is a sense of humility that comes with acting on data rather than on personal seniority and clout.[11]

Rising from the wreckage of the old system: Human-centric focus

The Henry Ford management model of 100 years ago thrived on impersonality. It largely removed humans from its scientific equation – except as docile, do-as-told cogs in the wheel. People were resources – not actors or drivers of change and certainly not leaders. In reality, the workplace is a deeply social space where individuals meet, learn, relate to and support each other, make sense of things and create their own personal as well as collective narratives and stories. Whereas top-down leadership almost solely recognized executives' rational and logical side, today's successful organizations are vibrant precisely

10   Miller, J. 2013.

11   Ferguson, R.B., 2013.

because they cultivate and draw on the uniquely human strengths of emotion, passion, imagination and empathy.

With the rise of digital, we cannot afford to go down the Fordist/Taylorist path again and reduce workers to inputs or to images on a screen. Thus far, organizations seem to recognize that: The 2020 flavors of remote work came complete with virtual coffee breaks, happy hours and watercooler chitchat. At the end of the day, it is people who do the heavy lifting in any organizational change. The idea of an organization's vision and mission always presupposed there was more to leadership than coercion (telling people what to do) or transactional exchange (buying their time). Studies show that inner commitment, also called intrinsic motivation, works better than external rewards such as bonuses.[12] The old adage is true – real change comes from within. Not only that, it comes to those who want to change much more often than those who, under pressure, feel that they have to change.

As a result, business leadership is increasingly becoming about relating to others, not demanding from them. The new, coaching style of leadership allows for candid and specific feedback including criticism. Combined with a sense of personal caring, these tough conversations produce what Kim Scott, a former executive at Google, Facebook and Apple, calls 'radical candor.'[13] In the bureaucratic order, managers often tried their best to sidestep these kind 'personal' and 'uncomfortable' conversations, keeping the peace but often at the cost of preventing individual employees from learning and growth.

Real leaders understand that the sweeping transformations, accelerated by Covid, are taking place at the intersection of technological and cultural change. According to Microsoft's CEO Satyam Nadella, the C in CEO stands for culture. A 2018

---

12   Ben-Hur, S. and Kinley, N., 2016.

13   Scott, K., 2019.

BCG survey involving more than 200 companies shows that addressing purpose, leadership and culture is the heart of the transformation effort and can increase odds of sustained impact by 50%.[14] 20th-century executives might have thought of culture as 'singing and dancing'. Some were even fond of the dictum, "When I hear the word 'culture', I reach for my gun." The concept sounded so antithetical to the serious business of management. Today, CEOs live and breathe cultural refresh and cultural renewal in their firms.

Culture in this sense needs to be visible and purposeful. It comes with its own rituals, myths and symbols. Eiji Toyoda would still come into his office in his nineties, devoting many of the visits to discussions with his younger successors. It wasn't because he couldn't 'let go'. Rather, he was exercising his leadership role as a 'keeper of the culture' by building an organizational memory that supported and reinforced the Toyota brand of valued behaviors.[15]

Millennials and Gen Z are shaping the future of work

The new ways of working and organizing we have seen emerge in recent years reflect many of the habits and preferences of a young workforce. But these are not just a nod to the millennials or an effort to retain them longer and in greater numbers: The old cubicle-land is ceding ground to squads and tribes. Powered by digital, speed and customer-centricity, the dynamics of these new teams emulates such quintessentially human qualities as empathy, creativity, iteration and spontaneity. Autonomous, cross-functional, cross-disciplinary teams are working hand in hand with customers. They are also pulling work towards themselves rather than having it pushed onto them from on high. In addition, members of Gen Z have a natural desire to connect with and learn from their peers, especially in online environments.[16]

---

14   Hemerling, J., Kilmann, J. and Matthews, D. 2018

15   Cossin, D. and Hwee, O.B., 2016.

16   Workforce Partnership Staff 2019.

Many companies have come to the realization that what they achieved in customer-centricity works just as well with internal customers, i.e., employees. So do the instruments of marketing and market research such as journey maps and persona development. As your business nudges towards new levels of flexibility and resilience, doesn't your human capital deserve the same attention that you accord to customers? It does, and that's why mapping and designing employee experience is now a valid and vibrant aspect of management change.[17]

The future of work goes hand in hand with the future of education

It was more than 40 years ago that Woody Allen said, in his movie Annie Hall: "Those who can't do, teach. And those who can't teach, teach gym." During the same time, universities around the world embarked on a huge shift from 'elite' institutions to gateways to higher education as geared for the masses. The field of education – itself a messy mix of history, identity, policy (but also politics) and economics – has been pulled in all sorts of directions ever since. With more stakeholders getting involved every decade, educators have commented that "everyone's an expert on education."

Whatever the face of 21st-century education, graduates ultimately want to a make a living and pay off their study loans. This particular space – of skills, employability, employment and job creation – has been dynamic and exciting, but also full of visible fissures that policymakers struggle to address. E.g. unemployment rate among Malaysia's university graduates has remained stubbornly high, at three times the national average – a troubling outcome when considering that education has for many years eaten up more than 20%

---

17   Plaskoff, J., 2017.

of the national budget (US$15 billion in 2020).[18]

Entering the new millennium, the debates raged on what it would take to fashion a new space that could merit the label of '21st-century learning.' The health crisis of 2020 brought these issues to a head, encouraging even more soul searching on what education in the next decade should be about and how it should be delivered. Challenging the status quo had never been more important. Beyond the easy mantra of 'distance learning', the act of temporarily abandoning the physical classroom has spurred a lot of other, more important reinvention.

As former US president Obama explained at a ConnectED to the Future event, "In a country where we expect free wifi with our coffee, the least we can do is expect that our schools are properly wired." But that is just the infrastructure part of the problem. To reconfigure what education is about, it is useful to ask fundamental questions like, what is school for? With blurred lines between traditional classroom education, home schooling and online learning, what is it that students take away? What is it they miss when schools are closed during a public health crisis? For many years, the pragmatic answer had to do with employability and skills. But just as there are many new directions in learning, the equation of learning and its outcomes and objectives also continues to evolve. New technologies including AI are unlikely to lead to the unsettling predictions of mass unemployment. But they will certainly require the redefinition of most occupations and requisite skills.[19]

In a world where software code itself is disappearing and many domains may soon take on a post-digital garb, real learning skills are seen as going beyond technologies and job descriptions. It is understood, albeit often intuitively,

---

18   nst.com.my

19   ozobot.com

that students will do well to work on their self-awareness, comfort with ambiguity and lateral and vertical collaboration skills. Another way of putting it is achieve goals, work effectively with others, manage emotions. All of these boil down to building trust, which is why character traits have made it to the list of what schools are supposed to shape, as well as soft skills and life skills.

What do young professional programmers have to say about job interviews and employability in general?

- With little or no formal work experience, candidates can impress interviewers with their school and personal projects, especially if they publicize them on GitHub, GitLab or Bitbucket.

- During interviews, they are expected to come up with a solution, even if it's not a flawless solution and takes a healthy amount of 'thinking out loud.'

- It doesn't hurt to show enthusiasm and passion about one's past efforts, as well as a knack for grappling successfully with non-technical, people and workplace problems.

The magic word: Impact

Ultimately, skills, knowledge and habits won't stick unless they share a deep connection with the learner's own world. Real, active learning happens when students not only listen, but also absorb and, crucially, form their own impressions and meaning of the material. That is what the modern school encourages students not only to learn but to showcase and apply what they learned. Terms like 'creativity' may sound like old hat and are not always easy to visualize. But a simple community project will spur students to find and frame a problem; present it to others; and piece together a solution. Each of these steps calls for creativity, teamwork, and critical thinking.

Tomaš Baťa

In 1929, thanks to shoemaking tycoon Tomáš Baťa (1876 – 1932; 'the Henry Ford of central and eastern Europe'), the town of Zlín, Czechoslovakia became one of the centers of the country's education reform. The goal was to prepare students for professional but also citizen roles in a democratic society. Learning was anchored in problem solving and practical projects that resonated with children's own life experience and were tailormade for their age and capability. Students learned about planning, sharing responsibilities and teamwork.

Experts have pointed out that the ability to make an impact requires 'propositional and experiential knowledge', not just textbook formulas. If this sounds like a can of worms, that's because it is – but it's a can of worms we must urgently open and tackle. We will find ourselves on a journey where we will have to think deeply about relevance (Syed Hussein Alatas[20]); about context, cultural values and unique ways of knowing; about empirical explorations; and about learning and research outcomes (the real ones, not just those we wrote up in a report, as if writing something down actually made it happen). If we examine these categories – and very few of us do that in the day-to-day – we may come away with sound ideas on how to 'do better by doing differently.'[21]

Metrics: Friend or foe?

Say 'impact', and we hear 'measure.' But what exactly do we measure, and how? Despite the modern world's obsession with rankings and 'what gets measured, gets done', we cannot allow education and university rankings to become a religion. Especially in developing countries, educators have voiced concerns

---

20   Alatas, S.H., 2000.

21   Kraemer-Mbula, E., Tijssen, R., Wallace, M.L. and McClean, R., 2019.

that a single-minded pursuit of good rankings and broader 'excellence' may in reality discourage internal debates on what direction a school should choose to deliver the best results for its students and other stakeholders. To quote Charles Malik again: The Greeks, more than any other people, displayed an irrepressible and unbounded passion for the exercise of reason and an incredible curiosity to investigate and know everything; and the university is nothing if it is not the home of free inquiry and unfettered curiosity. "All knowledge is of the universal," proclaimed Aristotle, and this is precisely the inalienable principle of the university. By knowledge Aristotle means scientific knowledge. Thus, from the beginning, the horizon of thought envisaged by the Greeks was the whole of mankind; they lived and thought in the presence of the unity of the human mind.[22]

Furthermore, in many fast-growing education markets, schools have plunged headlong into a numbers game of 'the more the merrier' – the more students they enroll, the more government funding is set to be coming their way. Needless to say, inflation is quick to set in. Interestingly enough, once quality suffers, quantity is sure to follow: In some EU countries, student dropout rates range from 50% to 80%. And not just among starry-eyed freshmen: They apply equally to undergraduate and postgraduate programs including doctorates, and sciences as well as humanities.[23]

For these schools and their government sponsors, measuring the effectiveness of every dollar or euro spent is clearly not a question of prestige or media relations anymore. It is the only way to prevent a colossal waste of taxpayers' money. And, in fact, an indicator as simple as value for money may just be the starting point. In 2021, Greece is set to roll out a set of metrics to gauge how its tertiary education players are stacking up. It will include parameters like the

---

22   Malik, C.H., 1982.

23   D'Hombres, B., 2007.

number of active students per program, annual spending per student, and the number of staff on short-term contracts. By 2022, 20% of state funding will be tied to performance outcomes in strategic areas chosen by the institutions, such as research activity or the number of international students.[24]

In Australia, starting in 2020, graduate employment outcomes are to be the most important factor under the performance-based funding model for universities.[25] Universities will receive a certain amount of government funding based on four performance measures: student drop-out rates; participation of indigenous, lower socioeconomic status and regional and remote students; student satisfaction with the university experience; and employment outcomes. Meanwhile, a report by the UK Institute for Fiscal Studies on the earnings of graduates in England provided further evidence of a deepening institutional divide, with its striking finding that at 23 unnamed universities, median earnings for male graduates 10 years after graduation were less than those of non-graduates.[26] This shows that many students are unlikely to go on to well-paid professional careers yet have accumulated student debts similar to those of their more fortunate peers.

Across the Atlantic, the escalation of study loans and prohibitive study fees has led many US historic colleges to downsize. For cities like Boston, whose small colleges have been reported to be on the verge of collapse, these developments could change the face of the city forever.[27] For all the criticism that has been directed in recent years at US colleges and especially liberal arts colleges, historically they have been pioneers in guiding students to find their voice in classroom discussions and debates. To do well in a class takes strong 'class participation', i.e. consistently

---

24   Ekathimerini (2020).

25   Jackson, D. and Bridgstock, R. (2019).

26   universityworldnews.com

27   bostonmagazine.com

coming up with fresh perspectives and independent opinions, coupled with critical thinking (the old adage of "use your sources, don't let your sources use you") and clear, analytical writing – no ifs or buts about it.

Learning for social and technological change

The talk of 'future-ready' schools and learning didn't start with Covid-19. There has been a growing realization since the late 1990s that the 21st century would demand a new way of handling information and knowledge. The idea of evolution in higher education originated even earlier, in the 1960s: It distinguished between three forms of higher education: (1) elite – shaping the mind and character of a ruling class which was getting ready to assume elite roles in society; (2) mass – transmission of skills and preparation for a broader range of technical and economic roles; and (3) universal – adaptation of the 'whole population' to rapid social and technological change.[28] The prediction has turned out remarkably accurate: As of 2020, the global rate of enrolment in higher education stands at 36%. That means developed countries are very near the envisaged 50% rate of universal higher education.

Reflecting the focus on talent and technology, and extending it further, the 2020 edition of GTCI was dedicated to Global Talent in the Age of Artificial Intelligence. The main questions it raised from a talent perspective include: What skills need to be developed to allow humans to take full advantage of the advances in AI, and how can those skills be provided, acquired, and updated?

The main issue on the supply side is: What can one reasonably expect from new and future AI capabilities in terms of recruitment, human resources management, and the enhancing of current and future human skills?

---

28   Trow, M., 1973.

Additionally, a specialized chapter in the report, New Skills for Augmenting Jobs and Enhancing Performance with AI, by Dimitris Bertsimas and Theodoros Evgeniou, discussed AI in the context of the types of skills that some describe as the 'missing middle': This is the broad area of skills that are required for hybrid tasks to be exercised jointly by humans and machines. Drawing on research by Daugherty and Wilson, the report foresees fruitful mutual contributions between humans on one hand and machines on the other through hybrid activities.[29] The skills that currently occupy the missing middle include:

- Rehumanizing time through better work-life balance and removing 'busyness' from day-to-day work

- Responsible, skillful, progressive introduction of AI as socially acceptable

- Developing and executing on a clear vision of the future of work in the organization

- Integrating human and AI judgement

- Intelligent interrogation, i.e., guiding AI onto paths where it can be the most helpful

- Bot-based empowerment, with AI agents granting employees 'superpowers'

- Holistic melding – working with AI in a congenial way, as if it were an extension of one's own persona or physical body

- Enhancing AI's ability for deep learning and vice versa

- Reimagining processes and business models in a way that makes them genuinely AI-enriched, as opposed to simply automated.

---

29   Daugherty, P.R. and Wilson, H.J., 2018.

Chapter 4

The new landscapes, spaces and voices of talent innovation

"The impossible takes a little longer."

Anonymous

Chapter 3 showed that we are getting a good handle on measuring, interpreting and increasingly predicting global trends in technology, innovation and talent development. In aggregate, these trends are producing new types of vibrant landscapes, spaces and players even in previously improbable corners of the world. Open innovation, i.e. companies casting the net wide in search of partners who could provide cutting-edge R&D, ideas and improvements to products, services and business models – has been with us for a few decades. Coupled with the 2020s widespread push into remote working and online collaboration platforms, the result is a geography of innovating anywhere, any time. Who are the new groups of players in this landscape?

As more and more entrepreneurial projects occur on a virtual platform and pursue a tech-based opportunity, digital entrepreneurs have carved out a sizable niche for themselves. Large numbers of college graduates or youngsters with a few years of experience and innovative minds are entering the digital space. They take advantage of the digital and content-rich social web that has given us new tools and marketing techniques. They apply these tools and techniques in a spirit of urbanity and openness to new solutions. Young people are also comfortable with digital project management tools and systems. In addition, they are strong in networking, online and offline, and asking for support. At the same time, digital ventures are finding homes within a growing number of platforms, from incubators through VC hubs to corporate collaboration engines.

Any entrepreneurs are by definition risk-takers with a great propensity for relying on what is described as entrepreneurial self-efficacy. They share a sense of optimism that borders on overconfidence. For digital entrepreneurs in today's era of open innovation and talent mobility, the world is their playground.

Meero, Agora and Kayrros

AI-powered image and video production startup Meero has developed a revolutionary professional photography solution. With the help of AI, an image is edited in a few seconds, a process which usually takes hours for a photographer. Uber, Just Eat, LVMH and Accor are just some of the companies which use Meero to optimize their photography process.

Founded in 2019, startup Agora launched a new social commerce platform for the beauty industry. The Agora app allows beauty fans to monetize their talent by creating and sharing video content that links directly to products from their favorite beauty brands.

Kayrros is an advanced data analytics company that helps global energy market players make informed trading, investment, and operational decisions. Using satellite imagery, natural language processing, Internet of Things, and machine learning, combined with in-house energy expertise, systems developed by Kayrros make it easier to predict oil and gas consumption, production, transport and storage.

Social entrepreneurs

Not long ago, the definition of entrepreneurship was 'making it big'. Business schools were competing in designing courses on 'How to turn a million-dollar business into a billion-dollar business'. Reality TV shows like The Apprentice glamorized the aggressive cut and thrust of business tycoons and sold the idea that business was about excess and making ruthless decisions.

By contrast, young entrepreneurs today are increasingly drawn to the concept of social entrepreneurship. They are aware of social and environmental issues and look upon enterprises as organizations with the legitimacy and the potential to address these problems. Social entrepreneurship thus combines the passion and drive for forming new ventures with the objective to improve the wellbeing of a selected social group or segment. Companies set up by social entrepreneurs have been observed to combine the efficiency, innovation, and resources of profit-making entrepreneurs with the passion, values, mission and concerns of nonprofit organizations.[1]

Alan, from Singapore

Founded in 2016, Alan is a digital health insurance platform, offering transparent pricing and policies to make healthcare more accessible.

Unlocking frictionless, fair and friendly healthcare for everyone, Alan was the first independent health insurance company in France since 1986. The startup distributes its own health insurance plans to both companies and individuals, providing a delightful health experience, beautifully designed tools, and wellness coverage (meditation, etiopathy, osteopathy). Currently, Alan covers more than 76,000 members, and has grown its team to 200 people.

Box continued on next page

---

1   Smith, W.K., Gonin, M. and Besharov, M.L., 2013.

Box continued from previous page

Attracting interest from investors including Singapore's Temasek global investment fund, by 2020 Alan raised more than 125 million euros in startup investment.

Social entrepreneurs connect their activities to broader societal efforts such as improving a community's quality of life; they often look for ways to reduce the negative effects of business stakeholders; and act as a multiplier of social impact. Overall, social entrepreneurs seek to balance the creation of financial, social and environmental wealth.[2]

Data specialists and digital entrepreneurs

As digital natives, many young people are drawn to work that involves creating digital assets such as content, design and portfolios. They can promote their skills as programmers or as experts in creating data visualizations and dynamic user experiences, as well as specialists in digital marketing including content marketing, marketing automation, social media marketing, and SEO. Those with extra ambition go on to set up digital startups that receive incubator, angel, and series A, B, and C funding, which allows them to build and expand digital enterprises. Others make a living from nothing more than their laptops. According to a 2019 study by Upwork, 57 million Americans describe themselves as freelancers. A large portion of this number leverage the power of the internet to market and deliver their services. Some experts have suggested that even before machine learning and AI penetrate all areas of life, digital living and digital entrepreneurship are already unfolding before our eyes as the next industrial revolution.

---

2   Zahra, S.A. and Wright, M., 2016.

ClickDo, from marketing to education

ClickDo grew from one freelance SEO consultant to a digital marketing agency. After graduating from university, ClickDo's present-day CEO Fernando Raymond delved into books about business and technology and came across an article in Forbes magazine titled Search Engine Optimization (SEO) is The Future.

The first clients paid a small monthly fee for his SEO services. Once the agency gained momentum, he joined forces with a self-taught web designer and a student of computer science. Together they were able to build a business website and add new services. To train staff in digital skills, over time they also set up ClickDo Academy online courses for SEO and digital marketing.[3] Today, ClickDo operates from offices in London's Canary Wharf and bills itself as a top Digital Marketing, SEM. PPC AdWords & Digital PR company.

In the corporate world, businesses are drowning in data from customers and ecosystem partners. Unsurprisingly, data scientists who can process, critically examine, interpret, and present the data are in high demand across industries. Companies that have adopted agile methodologies and transformed their workforce into tribes, chapters and squads often staff the majority of the squads with data analysts. Many of these positions have to be filled with candidates from overseas, indicating that data-related domains will be a jobseeker's market for years to come.

3   Young, J. 2018.

Digital social entrepreneurs

Merging technology with a social purpose is the domain of digital social entrepreneurs. In the past, these entrepreneurs were mainly niche players who experimented with using technology to address social issues, often in developing countries. Today, many startups seek to take a stand on social issues and reach a newer, more socially conscious audience. Digital, mainly social media, is their voice. The mushrooming of pro-social or socially minded, digitally-savvy up-and-comers has given rise to what some refer to as the social impact industry. Digital technologies allow these entrepreneurs new opportunities to tackle complex social problems and, importantly, not just point out issues but suggest creative solutions, often at scale, which thanks to creative ways of deploying technology may be within reach.

On top of wishing to do good, there are practical, technical aspects that digital social entrepreneurs must consider. Increasingly, those seeking to create social impact must be comfortable with a variety of digital tools and platforms. Supporting a social cause and communicating that support requires not only conviction but also familiarity with and proficiency in Facebook Ads, Google AdSense, Google Analytics, WordPress, Chatfuel, CrowdTangle, BuzzSumo, and other digital tools. Indeed, the modern-day equivalent of handing out flyers is mastery of a host of activities: Podcasts, customer discovery, digital content creation, small-dollar fundraising, consumer products, sponsored content, in-person events, ambassador programs, local or national organizing, online advertising, business model generation, distributed organizing, and influencer networks, as well as conducting technical training.

Advocating social change also takes a lot of numerical power, mainly the ability to analyze data and work with large spreadsheets. Meetings and discussions among social digital entrepreneurs revolve around social and political insights, and these may be derived from A/B testing. The internet has connected social entrepreneurs to a national and global audience – but understanding how to engage with that audience and what topics resonate with it takes numbers – from recent CTRs (click-through rates) to target CPAs (cost per action such as form submission). With digital, the business community in general has seen the line between thinkers and doers blur or disappear altogether: Forward-thinking CEOs regularly spend time on the frontline, e.g. fielding calls in a customer support center. For social enterprises, the lines between creative and technical input have similarly blurred. What matters is getting things done – and that may include bits and pieces of working independently or with a team, often remotely and virtually via videoconferences; working on one's own projects as well as thought partnering and learning from colleagues from diverse backgrounds.

Independent information can be free and financially sustainable

Revolution English is a subscriber-supported, nonprofit news media organization that exists to serve and empower immigrants in the United States. It has developed a financially self-sustainable model for providing free online English lessons to over one million immigrants, and also providing resources to get better jobs, immigration assistance, and advocacy opportunities. Revolution English is funded by subscriber donations as well as limited number of mission-aligned foundations, including the Four Freedom Funds Technology Media Initiative.

Creating social impact with the aid of digital platforms today has its own version of the Academy Awards. The Shorty Social Good Awards honor the agencies, brands and other industry players behind the best and most innovative work on social media and digital channels, campaigns, websites and applications. Winners of the fifth edition in 2020 included a 12-hour TikTok streamathon that raised more than $2 million for charities.

All of these pro-social activities have been powered with the 'old' internet which is about exchanging information. Imagine the possibilities that will come with the internet's next incarnations such as the Internet-of-Value: Just like data today changes hands at the speed of light, an internet of value, based on distributed ledger systems like blockchain, is expected to enable transactions and payments in real time and across global networks. Tough to imagine just a few years ago, the Covid health crisis has pushed the world closer to a stage where production, supply and demand, communications, payments, health, education and social interactions as well as other areas entail new kinds of electronic identification, transacting and payments.

For the time being, young digital citizens have flocked to new platforms and capabilities such as crowdfunding through websites and social networking platforms. They support crowdfunding projects because they believe that their contribution will make an impact. Today's crowdfunding ranges from equity investment to P2P lending, reward-based, donation-based and hybrid crowdfunding models. YouTube has also been home to a sponsorship market, monetizing content and providing brand partnerships and brand integration.

Smart cities as ideal testbeds for new ideas

Most of these new interactions and permutations of social, digital and talent innovation take place in smart cities. Smart cities apply technology to enhance the benefits and simultaneously reduce the shortcomings of urbanization. They outperform other cities in terms of indicators such as quality of life, mobility, safety, and competitiveness. They are described as livable as well as lovable:[4] Smart cities keep their sights fixed on the future while treasuring their past. A smart city tells a story of its forefathers and the generations of workers, merchants and migrants whose skill, effort and industriousness have made the city what it is today.

---

4   Bris, A., Cabolis, C. and Lanvin, B. eds., 2019.

For thousands of years, cities and the surrounding regions have been where the action is in terms of commerce, knowledge and opportunity in general. It was in the Mediterranean city-states that the main engines and institutions of capitalism were born during the 12th and 13th centuries: Merchant banks, insurance companies, newspapers, but also universities, museums, and art galleries. The instruments these communities created would lead to the accumulation of capital that was to produce maritime explorations (the Age of Discovery) and technological innovation including the printing press. Their urban spirit, regional mindset, openness to trade, and a systematic preoccupation with progress proved to be the mix of which the Renaissance was born.

Crucially, these prosperous cities never looked inward or sought to isolate themselves. Instead, they engaged in lively interactions with each other. As early as the late 1100s, Northern Europe's Hanseatic League emerged as a confederation of merchant towns all across the Baltic region as well as Northwestern and Central Europe.

By contrast, the majority of nation states have been a modern creation: Some emerged in the 19th and 20th centuries out of the wreckage of old, dynastic empires. Others were political projects, cobbling together dozens of small, previously self-ruled cities, principalities and duchies. For instance, upon modern Italy's unification in 1860, it is reported that only 8% of the population could understand the official language.

The political scientist historian Benedict Anderson (1936 – 2015) talked about nation states as 'imagined communities':[5] As individuals growing up in modern society, we have been conditioned to identify as Indian, Moroccan, German etc. Yet throughout our lifetime we will never personally meet but the tiniest fraction of our country's fellow citizens. The bonds that tie us with

---

5   Anderson, B., 2006 [1983].

them are largely imagined, virtual, fictitious: They include media images, symbols, official narratives. They are not tangible or otherwise 'real' in that we don't live, breathe, and touch them on a daily basis. Anderson also explored how the nation state was 'logoized' through modern communications, i.e., drawn onto maps and other visual objects in ways that only the most recent handful of generations has experienced. In other words, whatever emotional allegiance countries may enjoy among their citizenry, the fact remains that they are abstract creations, and to participate in them we must suspend a lot of our disbelief, much like when we watch a film.

Underscoring the dynamism that is associated with cities has been their rapid growth: In 1950, one-third of the world population lived in cities. Half a century later, the proportion had expanded to one-half, and it is estimated that, by 2050, six billion people (that is, two-thirds of the world population) will live in cities. Currently the urban population of developing countries is projected to double in 30 years, going up from 2 billion in 2000 to 4 billion in 2030. Less than 10 years from now, most of the 'mega-cities' emerging from that process will be located in developing countries.[6]

Cities in the digital age

Cities have never ceded this considerable power they have accrued over the centuries as focal points of people's real, lived-in formative experiences and a source of great opportunities in education, employment, networking, and self-expression. As early as the 1990s, telecom networks and the early days of the internet were eagerly absorbed into new features of urban infrastructure.[7] These new, superior levels of connectivity blended with and built upon the existing presence of learning structures, capable human resources and private sector initiative to produce knowledge hubs, either within established urban

6   Lanvin, B. and Lewin, A., 2006.

7   Townsend, A.M., 2001.

communities or as greenfield variations, carving out brand new spaces that were custom-designed to spur innovation and productivity.

Some have called the unrelenting sense of creativity and power cities have continued to exert the 'revenge of geography': Just when, technically at least, the internet made it possible for talent, manufacturing facilities, supply chains, and service networks to be located 'anywhere', physical proximity once again asserted itself through the appearance of ICT hubs across India and complex combinations of talent in places such as the City of London. Overall, the dynamics of the ICT sector, and of ICT infrastructure and services in general, have reinforced rather than diminished the influence and roles of the local level in the overall process of globalization.

Learn, test, adapt: Grab's strategy during the Covid-19 lockdowns

Grab has been Southeast Asia's answer to Uber and a major player in the gig economy that has emerged in cities like Singapore, Bangkok and Kuala Lumpur. During the health crisis, tens of thousands of new drivers joined the platform to make up for their lost earnings from 'regular' day jobs. With passenger movements restricted, 150,000 drivers across the region started performing on-demand deliveries for the first time. The Grab driver app enabled them to toggle between ride-hailing and delivery requests.

The cities' merchants likewise needed a new way to reach customers. In March and April, about 80,000 small businesses joined the platform. Many had never sold online before, so Grab expedited the release of a self-service feature, making it easier for merchants to on-

Box continued on next page

Box continued from previous page

board themselves. According to Grab executives, "a massive sector of Southeast Asia's economy effectively digitized within a matter of weeks."[8]

A lot of the new merchants had previously accepted only cash payments, so Grab had to set them up for digital payments, a process made simpler because the company's financial unit, Grab Financial, already offers services like Grab Pay for cashless payments, mobile wallets, and remittance services.

Grab also released a new package of tools called Grab Merchant, which enabled merchants to register online businesses by submitting licenses and certification online and includes features like data analytics.

The challenge was scaling up its delivery services to meet the dramatic increase in demand by consumers: Part of Grab's Covid-19 strategy involved collaborating with local municipalities and governments in different countries to make deliveries more efficient. For example, it worked with the Singaporean government to expand a pilot program, called GrabExpress Car, originally launched in September, that enabled more of Grab's ride-hailing vehicles to be used for food and grocery deliveries. Previously, many of those deliveries were handled only by motorbikes.

The situation in each of Grab's markets – Singapore, Cambodia, Indonesia, Malaysia, Myanmar, Philippines, Thailand, and Vietnam – is evolving. But the company is preparing for an uncertain future by modeling different scenarios, taking into account potential re-closings, and long-lasting changes in both consumer and merchant behavior. The company is expanding GrabExpress, its same-day courier service, and adapting technology originally created for ride-pooling to help drivers plan pickups and deliveries more efficiently.

Box continued on next page

---

8   Shu, C. 2020.

Box continued from previous page

Meanwhile, Grab has teamed up with Microsoft to launch three training and development programs that will empower up to 5,000 driver and delivery partners as well as 250 digitally inclined students to help them secure IT-related job and traineeship opportunities.

Driver and delivery partners wanting to upskill their digital knowledge will have free access to Microsoft's e-learning digital literacy modules via the GrabAcademy in the Grab partner app, and those keen on beginning a software development career can also sign up for an eight-month train-and-place program.

A separate pilot program with Singapore Polytechnic is also available for tertiary students, where they will learn more about artificial intelligence and its application to real-world scenarios.

"As the leading technology player in the region, we have a role to play in improving digital inclusiveness and literacy in the communities we serve, as well as in creating more pathways for our driver and delivery partners who are keen to capture these opportunities," said Yee Wee Tang, managing director of Grab.[9]

The 'Introduction to Digital Literacy' program comprises six modules on basic computing and digital skills content such as internet usage, online productivity and communications tools, online security and safety, among others. Participants who finish this program will receive a certification from Grab and Microsoft.

The program has already been introduced in Indonesia and Vietnam, with more than 439,600 certifications issued to Grab's partners in both markets since February 2020.

Grab will eventually extend the program to driver and delivery partners in Cambodia, Malaysia, Myanmar, Philippines, and Thailand.

---

9   Howell, P. 2020.

On the physical level, the expansion of cities around the world has raised questions about their future capacity to sustain this type of growth while maintaining adequate levels of production and delivery of key public services such as water, transport, electricity, sanitation, education, and containment of crime and pollution. There is, however, another side to this equation, often overlooked. It relates to the emerging role of cities (and of subnational entities generally) to become global players – as attractors of foreign investment, competitiveness hubs, and/or platforms for the combination of local and international components of global production and supply chains.[10]

For the time being, central governments have been delegating an increasing number of their traditional responsibilities to subnational entities such as states, regions, municipalities, and cities. Therefore, cities have increasingly acted as global players, designing and implementing their own policies and strategies to attract investment and carving out their share of benefits from the emerging global economy. Today's cities have emerged not only as key players in global competition but as central actors who have been spreading and shaping the processes of globalization itself.

The idea of 'smart cities' is one of communities that maximize the benefits and successfully manage the downsides and risks of rapid urbanization. The choices we need to make today about what makes a city smart matter because the momentum of technological innovation will continue to rise in the near future. That will introduce us to new opportunities in addressing pending global challenges in areas such as climate change, inequalities, health, and education.[11] Cities also need to be aware of whether they are successfully promoting inclusive prosperity: to take one example, it was found that between 2010 and 2015, only 11 of the United States' 100 largest city areas generated inclusive prosperity for their residents.[12]

---

10   Lanvin, B. and Lewin, A., 2006.

11   IMD Smart City Index

12   picsaindex.com

All along, cities have continued to adapt and to up their game. Twenty years ago, the smaller-sized capital cities of emerging Europe – Vilnius, Riga, Ljubljana, Bratislava – were ridiculed in many quarters for their absence of major international airports but also, in some cases, such 'basic' trappings of global lifestyle as a McDonald's outlet. Today, as the emphasis has shifted to all things green and sustainable, these places' location on railway and river networks rather than air travel routes has emerged as a plus point. So has their compact size, walkability and safety.

European cities have also actively integrated into a 'Europe of the regions', building physical and other links with their peers in neighboring countries. This vision of regions rather than nation-states as the continent's building blocks emerged shortly after WWII. The architects of postwar Europe realized early on that for the necessary healing and recovery to take place, they would have to draw on cross-border and people-to-people networks rather than 'official', diplomatic and other contacts at the level of central governments.

Hopping from city to city: Digital nomads

In one of their latest incarnations, cities – and particularly medium-sized cities – have fashioned themselves as hubs for digital nomads and other transient, remote workers. Digital nomads are people who are location-independent and use technology to perform their job. Flexible, light travelers, they are sociable and friendly; they aim for success and a healthy work-life balance. Armed with a laptop and a backpack, they are always on the road, exploring new destinations with the help of job opportunities, scholarships and volunteer projects. They commonly include web developers, graphic designers, copywriters, movie editors, digital marketing specialists, photographers, journalists, bloggers, translators and language instructors but also tantric healing gurus and internet poker players.

Female digital nomads and their formal and informal networks have also established themselves as a force to reckon with in the corporate world: Location-independent careers have offered many women the type of lifestyle and in many

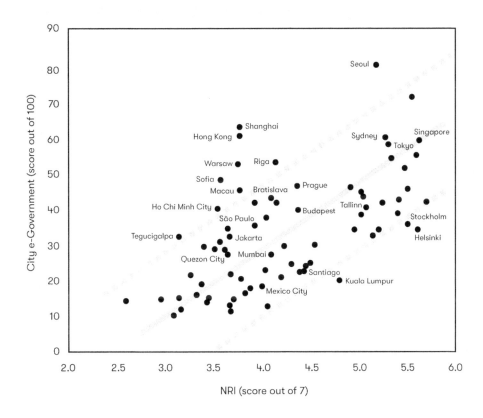

Figure 7: City e-Government vs Overall Network Readiness

cases balance between work and parenting that traditional employment rarely could. For Natalie Sisson, the concept is simple: "you design a business around your talents, skills and knowledge, that gives you the freedom to do all the things you want, when you want. Using online tools, technologies and systems, you can work in a way that sustains the lifestyle you want – whether that's having more time to play with your children or being able to travel the world"[13].

Partly in response to the global wave of digital nomading in recent years, there has been a growing body of relevant practical data, accessible through sites

13   Quoted from suitcaseentrepreneur.com

like Numbeo.com, NomadList.com and Expatistan.com. These allow for city-to-city comparisons regarding the cost of living, internet speed, ease of communication in English, availability of good-quality coworking, coliving and other colocation facilities, pedestrian safety, as well as quality of healthcare and transport etc. Equally important are considerations such as environmental quality but also the less tangible aspects including openness to foreigners, gender and racial tolerance.

On Nomad List, Bangkok, for example, is rated as follows: Pros – affordable to live; very safe; fast internet; lots of fun stuff to do; warm now and all year round; perfect humidity now; good air quality on average; Nomad List members liked going here; Nomad List members are here all year round; easy to make friends; very easy to do business; great hospitals; people can speak basic English; very safe for women; family-friendly; friendly to LGBTQ+. Cons: too hot all year round; feels crowded; quality of education is low; roads are very dangerous; freedom of speech is weak; not very democratic.

All in all, digital nomads have been drawn to what makes a city dynamic and vibrant. At the same time, they have shunned locales that have been a victim of their own past success and are now suffering from a skyrocketing cost of living, overcrowding and housing shortages. As could be expected based on these criteria, the process has produced some unlikely and previously little-known winners in this global game of remote work. New York, London, and Paris may top the rankings of exciting travel destinations. But when it comes to affordable living, working via cyberspace and networking with other nomads, it's places like Playa del Carmen, Mexico and Cluj, Romania that have been consistently topping the nomad charts over the years.

Estonia is launching a new Digital Nomad Visa for remote workers

Estonia has launched a Digital Nomad Visa that allows remote workers to live in Estonia and legally work for their employer or their own company registered abroad.

Digital nomads and remote workers have long faced ambiguity when working while they travel, often skirting the law by working while visiting a country with a tourist visa.

But since August 1, 2020, eligible location-independent workers can apply for the chance to come to Estonia to live for up to a year with peace of mind that they can legally work.

Estonia has already transformed the way a country serves people beyond its borders through programs such as e-Residency. Now with the Digital Nomad Visa, Estonia is transforming how people in the world choose to work.

While other countries like Costa Rica, Mexico, Portugal and the Czech Republic have introduced visas for digital nomads, so far these have primarily targeted freelancers. In contrast, the new Estonian Digital Nomad Visa (DNV) covers a broader range of digital nomads — in addition to freelancers, it also allows teleworking from Estonia if the person has a foreign employer or is a partner in a company registered abroad. This gives location-independent entrepreneurs from around the world a legitimate way to live and work in the country for up to a year.[14]

14   Hankewitz, S. 2020.

Responding to Covid challenges

Many existing, pre-crisis trends have been accelerated during the pandemic and are pushing cities to continue reinventing themselves. For instance, Silicon Valley saw an exodus of residents even pre-Covid, caused largely by escalating property prices, near-permanent traffic jams and persistently high rates of homelessness. As a result, startups have been moving away or have become 'fully distributed', with only their most important employees living in San Francisco and the rest spread across the world. Big Silicon Valley companies, including Facebook and Google, let employees work from home until the end of 2020. Twitter says they can do so indefinitely.[15]

Urban planning – the idea of a multitude of diverse actors prospering through invisible but shared systems and infrastructures – has captured the imagination of many players going through radical reorganization, including corporations. Similarly, cities' response to Covid-19 drew on their previous efforts in building urban resilience through place-based and people-centered approaches to digitalization, mobility, density, urban design and collaborative governance.[16]

The smart city recipe

Smart cities have been a bit of a paradox: They embed some of the highest hopes of mankind through the promise of harnessing technology for better lives and social harmony. For some, however, they could incarnate the fears of 'controlled lives' in some kind of panopticons governed by artificial intelligence and automated devices.[17] Nevertheless, if the last wave of globalization primarily swept the nation states, it is cities who are well and truly the modern-day global players. On an ever-greater scale, cities take on the functions and commitments that nations cannot and will not take on. In some countries, for instance, cities

---

have picked up the responsibilities in fighting climate change that their national governments have failed to take on or have walked back on supporting.

What is clearly emerging is that smart cities function at their best when they remain a crossroads of human flows; economic, trade and investment flows; flows of ideas and a keen awareness of history, i.e. how the community came to be the way it is today. The mix of compelling yet universal ingredients such as purpose, interplay of human and technological trends, and a strong dose of shaping perception and branding is here to stay as smart cities' enduring recipe.

Bilbao, Bizkaia: Successful revitalization, inclusive prosperity

Bilbao, with around 350,000 inhabitants, is the capital of Biscay and the economic, social, and cultural center of the Basque Country.

Due to the profound crisis in the 1980s that affected its fundamental economic sectors (metallurgy, steel and naval), the city needed to reinvent itself and face up to great challenges: high rates of unemployment, environmental and urban degradation, strong internal emigration, and the emergence of social marginalization issues.

Bilbao was able to achieve a transformation thanks to local political management as well as public-private and inter-institutional cooperation.

The city's success has been acknowledged on the world stage:

- Lee Kuan Yew World City Prize, 2010

- European Public Sector Award (EPSA), 2011

- World Mayor Prize bestowed on mayor Iñaki Azkuna (1943 – 2014), 2012.[18]

---

18   sustainabledevelopment.un.org

Why nurture these new spaces, landscapes, voices? Because history shows us they are vulnerable

Action at local level, particularly city level, will guide many of our efforts towards a better global future. Cities will likely do a lot more of the heavy lifting than they get credit for in the upcoming project of rebuilding globalization around a set of shared values (Chapter 6). These include environmental sustainability, better health and education, and reduced inequality, but also faith in a shared future.[19] As such, they deserve support as well as better understanding, particularly insights, new trends and good practices that are identified through systematic data collection and analysis. In that spirit, the 2020 GTCI particularly calls for stronger city-level data collection in terms of more business- and impact-oriented indicators such as ease of doing business, foreign direct investment (FDI), and number of patent applications.

In the 20th century, many of modernity's heroes ultimately became its victims. Urban centers that emerged as regional and global hubs between the turn of the century and WWII have often declined. As a result of international conflict or domestic political strife, their once unassailable positions have long been usurped by newcomers.

The smart cities of 100 years ago

Azerbaijan's capital Baku is the largest city on the Caspian Sea. Large-scale oil wells sprang up around Baku in the 1870s, attracting global investors including the Rothschilds and the Nobel Brothers company.[20] By the beginning of the 20th century, half of the oil

Box continued on next page

---

19 Key messages of NRI 2020.

20 Eyvazova, G. 2020.

Box continued from previous page

sold in international markets was extracted in Baku. A highly diverse hive of investment and activity, Baku became home to large communities of Azeri as well as Armenian, Jewish and Russian residents. The great prosperity of the time is still visible in the city's many ornate Belle Epoque palaces, mansions, theaters, and other structures. Yet with Azerbaijan perpetually caught in the crosshairs of Russo-Iranian rivalry, following the downfall of the Ottoman Empire, Baku was taken over by Bolshevik forces and declared capital of the Azerbaijan Soviet Socialist Republic, soon to be rolled into the Soviet Union.

Situated on the western bank of the waterway that is formed by the union of the Tigris and Euphrates rivers, Iraq's second largest city of Basra established itself after WWI as one of the most important commercial ports in the Arabian Gulf. Its shipping and trade links spanned all the way to East Asia, and the port's administrative buildings were described as among the most impressive in Iraq at the time. With the addition of a railway terminus and a civilian airport, Basra grew to become a sprawling city where multiple quarters competed for status.[21] In 1927, Imperial Airways launched regular flights on the Cairo-to-Basra route, using DH.66 aircraft. Aviation thus linked the city to other global travel hubs of the time such as Karachi, Rangoon, Hong Kong, Singapore, Entebbe, Nairobi and Dar es Salaam. Aviation also helped open the oil fields to the Anglo-Persian Oil Company, a forerunner of BP.

Meanwhile, Basra's old town enjoyed a reputation for luxury hotels, jazz bands and international entertainers. In the Oscar-winning 1940 Hollywood film The Thief of Bagdad, it is in Basra that the young sultan falls in love with the princess.

Box continued on next page

---

21   Visser, R. 2006.

Box continued from previous page

During WWII, it was through Basra as a major transshipment point that western Allies sent military supplies to the Soviet Union.

Known as the 'melting pot of the Gulf' and with a long history of Ottoman rule, Basra's political and mercantile priorities differed widely from those of the Iraqi state. As a result, in recent decades the city took the brunt of every war and political conflict that enveloped the modern Iraqi stage. During the 1980s Iran-Iraq War, its population is estimated to have fallen from close to a million to just over 400,000. The city's outskirts also saw heavy fighting during the early phases of the Iraq War of 2003.

Want to know the future? Support, partner with, get to understand these new players

Smart cities, digital nomads, digital social entrepreneurs, social impact players: These new movers and shakers combine current trends with what is coming – not only in work but also in mobility, communications, travel, parenting, and work-life balance. Engaging with them and getting to know them better should be a priority for businesses, national and local governments, and civil society organizations everywhere. If you want to catch a glimpse of the formulae that are very likely to transform your organization, this new landscape is a treasure trove of information, innovation ideas, and talent.

Many younger workers at more progressive employers were already working remotely from locations across the world before Covid-19, using Airbnbs as well as more specialized work-life lodging options, such as Outsite. Today, much of the professional world is shifting to remote and hybrid work arrangements. That makes the new spaces and new opportunities for young talent even more appealing.

In the meantime, new practices continue to set in. Quarantines are leading young people, especially digital nomads, to stay longer in one destination. Slow travel, rather than jumping on an airplane and trekking around 150 or 190 countries in quick succession, is becoming the way to experience the world in the 2020s. A Google search on 'slow travel' yields over a billion results in 0.6 seconds, with most of the top-rated links dated 2020. A younger cousin of the slow-food movement, slow travel is a more thoughtful approach to traveling. Measured by 'moments, not miles', it is about immersing oneself in local places, communities, culture and cuisines. Think Eat, Pray, Love for the digital age.

At the same time, professionals young and old, unshackled from cubicledom, want to live in smaller, affordable cities and closer to nature. In tandem, new disciplines of thought and management are emerging, such as remote leadership. Managing a team was always a valuable skill; now it is the ability and experience in building and leading teams that are scattered around the world while keeping them highly effective, motivated and productive that is sought after by many companies.

Covid has also unexpectedly reversed many long-standing migration flows: Across eastern Europe, hundreds of thousands of workers have left – voluntarily or otherwise – their employment in the UK, Germany, Netherlands and other countries and returned to their once sleepy and depopulated hometowns. Some are keen to resume their old life in the host countries, other are determined to stay at home for good. The majority came back with new language, tech and other skills. What they need is better opportunities to put those skills to good use.

Human-centric, courageous enough to venture into the unknown, using technology to address real issues faced by real people – those are the qualities shared by the new actors in the 2020s landscape of global talent and talent innovation. If we can learn to understand and support them better, and gauge their impact with more accuracy and foresight, it will not only humanize the ongoing acceleration of technology adoption, but also further energize the role of young talent in tomorrow's education, government and industry.

Innovative Metrics to build a human-centric future – The example of IMD's Smart City Observatory, and the Smart City Index

In 2018, the Institute for Management Development (IMD) and the Singapore University of Technology and Design (SUTD) decided to join forces to produce a human-centric quantitative tool to assess, benchmark and improve the performance of smart cities. The operating arms of those two high-level academic institutions were the Smart City Observatory and the Lee Kwan Yew Center for Innovative Cities, respectively. Since 2019, a unique Smart City Index has hence been produced annually, ranking more than 100 cities from all parts of the world.

The index is entirely based on citizens' perceptions. It covers a wide range of aspects of urban quality of life including air quality, fluidity of traffic and mobility solutions, waste management, safety, and access to services, to name only a few.

In addition to this annual ranking, the publication of the index is accompanied by a collection of case studies, with the aim of bringing context to the index, and rooting it in the reality of actual successes, failures and challenges of smart cities (or aspiring smart cities) from all parts of the world. The first collection of case studies was included in the 2019 award-winning book called Sixteen Shades of Smart; the second one was published at the end of 2021 under the title Cities in Times of Global Emergencies.

Box continued on next page

Box continued from previous page

As mentioned in the preface of that second volume, smart cities are typically the place where people, technology and innovation meet and attempt to shape a common desirable future. But there are many ways to be smart. Casting the bases of a more environmentally supportive urban future can be done in more than one way. Most smart cities are still in a phase of trial-and-error in this respect, and this is why comparative studies and exchanges of experiences among cities are so important. The pandemic has played the role of an accelerator in this regard, forcing cities' mayors and decision makers to adopt emergency measures when their citizens' lives were at stake.

Taking a longer-term perspective, smart cities will remain key testbeds for the deployment of new technologies, especially around artificial intelligence. Smart cities (and their citizens) will hence have a key role to play in shaping the laws and regulations that will be needed to ensure the prevalence of human-centric efforts over pure technological (and market) concerns.

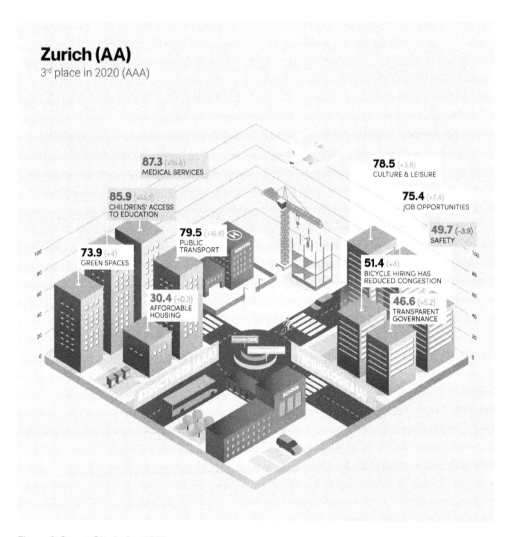

Figure 8: Smart City Index 2021

Chapter 5

Young values are the lifeblood of the new geographies of talent innovation

"Life is never made unbearable by circumstances but only by lack of meaning and purpose."

Viktor Frankl (1905 – 1997), author of Man's Search for Meaning[1]

Much of the literature about millennials and the millennial workforce is written as a lament. "How are we ever going to extract any utility out of these kids?", is the underlying sentiment. "They need constant reassurance; they live for Instagram posts and computer games; and there's no tearing them away from their phones." The books then go on to dish out dos and don'ts on how to make this workforce 'fit in' with the old, stable work environment.

In reality, that environment is no more. It may have been stable once upon a time – but it was stable in a rigidly bureaucratic and top-down way. Thriving on command and control, it treated workers as impersonal building blocks. The discussion we presented in Chapter 4 of this book highlighted that this old, hierarchical order is now a thing of the past. Globalization, digital, the rise of China – the confluence of these powerful forces has swept it away for good.

---

1   Frankl, V.E., 1985.

Let us be clear on that: The spaces, landscapes and geographies of business, tech and innovation that have replaced them (Chapter 5) are not here to accommodate young people. To work the way they were set up to work, they badly need an infusion of young perspectives, habits and values. The world has changed. Organizations are busy dismantling bureaucracy and hierarchy. In this new world, they need input and an outlook on life from young people, unencumbered by the old models which have long run out of relevance and usefulness. And they're in luck – because a firm set of values, a sense of purpose and a continual search for meaning are what defines the young generation, and in many cases sets it apart from its forebears.

Unlike their parents, young people don't think of material possessions and consumption as a source of validation and self-worth. They were never conditioned to expect that their material standard of living will be automatically higher than it was for the previous generation. Sure, at times they get criticized for being 'entitled', but it's not greed or a compulsive accumulation of property that captivates them.

By now it has become clear that millennials are seeking a new model of the meaningful life. They want to change the world by connecting to a higher good, not through violence or drugs or counterculture. They demand to be a part of something that is bigger than the self, personal gain or company profit. They seek a sense of connection to society as a whole. Their aspirations may not always be clearly articulated but they bring to mind the following quote: "Doing the right thing, when required, is a calling from on high. Do it boldly, do as you believe, do as you are."[2]

---

2   Nonaka, I., & Takeuchi, H. 2011, May.

Young people are looking for – and finding – happiness at work

By 2025, the millennial generation will represent 75% of the workforce.[3] As we mentioned in Chapter 2, millennials have steadily challenged the way organizations work. They want to make a difference, experience the thrill of making things happen, and see tangible outcomes of their effort. Beyond the paycheck, young workers are looking for meaning and fulfillment in their employment.[4] In a world where concepts like people-centric, customer-centric, 'We > I' have taken the workplace by storm, they want to know that their effort has made a customer's life easier and better. Some bring their sense of empathy to a point where they describe it as love.

Young people expect to have their voice heard; to be treated as an 'internal customer'; and to have room at work for qualities such as imagination and emotion. Increasingly, they are motivated by higher-order, self-actualization needs.[5] They are driven by an interest or enjoyment in doing the work itself and are motivated from within rather than by external pressures or a desire for reward. They want to feel trusted, not controlled and monitored. Trust gives them a secure base so that they can take risks and constantly improve and innovate. In consequence, they are drawn to employers who stand for things that resonate with their personal view of themselves; the company's success or failure then becomes their own.[6]

Young workers refuse to leave their personal hopes and values at home. To accept a job with the sole purpose of paying bills sounds like vacant irresponsibility, soulless and mercenary. In this sense they echo what 1940s writer Anaïs Nin (1903 – 1977) noted in her diary, "There is an ugliness

---

3   Prossack, A. 2018.

4   Wootton, C. and Grundy, J., 2018.

5   Maslow, A., 1965.

6   Higgs, M. and Lichtenstein, S., 2011.

in being paid for work one does not like." Instead, they are motivated by empathy and by social and ethical ideals. Those who are drawn to religious values recognize that these endorse a person's intrinsic worth, regardless of social or career status.

Remarkably, many have emerged unscathed from a childhood marked by 'helicopter parenting' whose central message was, "You are my investment; now watch me maximize the return on that investment." Consumerism died on the vine; it just doesn't appeal to them. Years ago it gave way to edifying experiences, quality leisure, creativity and other types of psychological value-add. And for many, sticking to their guns has paid off: A survey by Happiness Works found that just 8% of 18- to 34-year-olds consider themselves to be unhappy at work, less than half the number from the 35 to 49 bracket and those over 55.[7]

Science of happiness

The new generation's quest for happiness and fulfillment, even in the context of the corporate setting of goals, deadlines and KPIs, hasn't gone unnoticed. It has been the main factor behind the rise of positive psychology, mindfulness in the workplace, and the emergence of happiness and well-being as a scientific discipline. Given that happier workers are not only more productive but almost directly translate into happier customers, everyone – employers, workers, academics – has a stake in understanding the happiness factors better. In the past few years, some universities including UC Berkeley have launched open online courses on the Science of Happiness.[8]

Buddhist scholars have long pointed out that concepts such as 'loving kindness' are based on a thought of 'giving', whereas the standard international discourse

---

7   Martin, W. 2017.

8   Greater Good. (n.d.).

of laws and seeking protection of one's rights reflect a metaphor of 'taking'.[9] Today, a life-and-work philosophy of practicing kindness and gratitude is not just the product of spiritual domains or a matter of fashion. Increasingly, it is backed by scientific research as evidence of what the main factors are that make humans and particularly young individuals flourish. Among them: Working towards their personal and professional goals; but also coming to grips with emotional responses and triggers; learning how to stop dwelling on negative thoughts; and practicing gratitude by taking the time to reflect on the things they are thankful for.[10]

"Never cease to be amazed" (Gaston Bachelard)

"The whole universe comes to contribute to our happiness when reverie comes to accentuate our repose. You must tell the man who wants to dream well to begin by being happy. Then reverie plays out its veritable destiny; it becomes poetic reverie and by it, in it, everything becomes beautiful."[11]

Gaston Bachelard, The Poetics of Reverie: Childhood, Language, and the Cosmos (1960)

Bachelard (1884 – 1962) was a philosopher who devoted his study of poetics to the exploration of 'the remarkable psychic productivity of the imagination' and its relationship to happiness, memory and our sense of wonder.

---

9   Alatas, S.F., 2003.

10   Happify.com. (n.d.).

11   Bachelard, G., 1971.

Lifehacks, hackathons, sharing economy: The corporate world is absorbing young lingo

This mindset that doesn't treat material possessions as the be-all and end-all of human ambition has given rise to entire new segments of the economy and social life. Young people use technology and shared services as 'lifehacks' (you hack at it, without any overblown expectations, until it yields some utility). Why spend on auto insurance and road tax when a car-sharing ride is a click away? This doing-more-with-less approach has influenced nearly every industry. Even luxury segments – once synonymous with ownership of coveted, pricey goods – are busy experimenting with rental and subscription models. They have no choice; the new cohort of buyers aren't keen on hoarding outfits in the closet. As of 2019, the New York-based Rent the Runway online business, for example, was valued at $1 billion.[12]

Some of the world's biggest conglomerates are realizing that they, too, can 'hack' their way to incremental innovations and addressing strategic blind spots – in a fun, youthful and affordable format. In banking, Singapore's DBS bank has taken part in global innovation hackathon, with hundreds of teams form 70 countries competing to create the best customer-centric approach to cutting-edge digital services. The bank has also engaged 65 industry partners in finance, healthcare, retail and automobile through industry discovery workshops aimed at strengthening its digital ecosystem.[13]

How to channel this energy into long-term impact?

Young people have strong values and boundless energy, but they often lack inspiration and hope. In this light, what are the questions that should be on our minds today? How can we best support young minds' probing efforts with a creative vision, energy and ambition?

---

12   nytimes.com

13   Henderson, J., 2020.

- *Involve them directly*

Some companies struggle with two apparently unrelated problems: figuring out how to engage and motivate their workers; and crafting a response to changing market conditions. A few organizations have tackled both problems at the same time by creating a 'shadow board of millennials' – a group of non-executive employees that works with senior executives on strategic initiatives. The purpose? To leverage the younger groups' insights and to diversify the perspectives that executives are exposed to.[14]

In 2015, Gucci created a shadow committee made up of millennials under the age of 30[15] from different functional areas within the organization.[16] And it wasn't just window dressing: In the years that followed, Gucci recorded double-digit growth while some of its direct rivals stagnated. It became the star performer within its parent conglomerate Kering's stable of prominent luxury brands. The strategy of going beyond hiring influencers to actually listening to what young people have to say about fashion, luxury, sustainability and digital seems to have paid off.

Meanwhile, luxury juggernaut LVMH has launched a program called DARE (Disrupt, Act, Risk to be an Entrepreneur), bringing together executives and employees to submit radical business ideas that relate to themes such as green initiatives and the customer experience of tomorrow. The ideas are fine-tuned and pitched in fun-filled, rapid, three-day cycles that culminate in a handful of initiatives getting selected for execution. Thus DARE is designed to foster speedy innovation but also to bust the siloed culture of LVMH's individual Maisons.[17]

---

14   hbr.org

15   Jordan, J. and Sorell, M. 2019.

16   Munzenrieder, K. (2017).

17   lvmh.com

• *Step aside and give them space to lead*

Youths show Malaysia's lawmakers that virtual parliament is feasible

Frustrated with the fact that the country's parliament had not convened for any debate between December 2019 and July 2020, as well as with the government's refusal to migrate parliamentary sittings online, a group of Malaysian youths sought to demonstrate that a digital parliament was feasible.

The world's first-ever youth-led digital 'parliament' went live on Microsoft Teams. Some 222 youth representatives, mirroring the federal seats in Malaysia, convened for a two-day debate session to discuss and pass new 'laws' and 'policies' on economic and education issues affecting youth in the country via the online platform. The virtual parliamentary proceedings emulated an actual sitting including voting and passing of bills. The session was streamed live on 4 and 5 July 2020, recording more than 200,000 viewers for both days.

A total of 30 percent of the seats were represented by women while 64 percent of the East Malaysia seats were elected from indigenous communities. Youth with disabilities were also represented.

While the application was opened to Malaysians between the age of 15 and 35 years old, the average age of the 'elected' representatives was 21 years old. The idea of a digital parliament was met with an enthusiastic response, with nearly 6,300 young Malaysians applying for the 222 constituency seats. Of the total applications, more than 1,500 were submitted within 24 hours of opening the registration. The sitting was conducted in Bahasa Malaysia, the national language, with sign-language interpretations. It attracted a total of 88,000 views on Facebook, with 561 shares and 693 reactions.[18]

---

18   Gnaneswaran, D. (2020).

The previous chapter highlighted the role of smart cities in the new global geography of innovation. But without drawing out real feedback and ideas from youth, many 'smart city' projects run the risk of turning into technocratic dystopias run by government agencies and big-tech vendors. To breathe life into a smart-city project, ideas must be solicited from young people on how to improve city residents' lives; and how to extracts benefits from a city's digital transformation without creating a place of surveillance, exploitation and exclusion.[19] A rush to design and build the What without painstakingly studying and respecting the How and the Who will bring the city to a dead end of technology for technology's sake. Avoiding that scenario demands that young people:

- View the Charter for Smart Cities through a context-heavy, culturally, geographically and historically sensitive lens

- Be trained in critical assessment of technology, how it relates to cities and city life, and youth's role in urban environments

- Become hands-on with exchanging best practices that provide links between urbanism and technology.

Through active, direct communication, youth will learn how to use and balance theoretical inputs, training, workshops, discussions, reflection, planning, brainstorming and other interactive methods of learning. The ultimate goal will be to come up with a draft toolkit for action which will stimulate public debate on smart-city policies and influence local decision making.[20]

- *Affirm that the world needs values – any values*

Whether clearly defined or hidden from view, values and beliefs are at the core of our activity. They are the bedrock of individual lives as well as

---

19   cdnee.org

20   Ibid.

organizations. Because values express 'a truth,' in day-to-day situations they are acted on rather than observed. In fact, values are by definition so stable and enduring that most people will seldom articulate or try to clarify them unless they come across a visible contradiction or threat.[21]

Values are not just 'nice' – they are important as vehicles that help us transcend our narrow self and invest in something more permanent than personal or company profit. In the western world, one's private life is typically compartmentalized from one's professional life. That makes many people cautious about bringing their personal values and convictions to work with them. By contrast, in other parts of the world even business leaders are openly motivated by family, religious, patriotic and other values. Often it is the love of their community, school or country that energizes them far beyond monetary gain.

Former President Director of Indonesia Port Corporation (IPC), Richard J. Lino, known as 'Pak Lino', returned to the company after 20 years in the private sector. On the list of company values put forward by Pak Lino upon his return to IPC, 'nationalism' was ranked near the top, right behind 'not [being] afraid of change.' In his own words: "What motivated me to take over the transformation of a slow-moving, government-run company? Personally, it is not about money or glory. I want to contribute. Ever since I was a child, I was thinking about the sea that surrounds us and how one day this may allow me to do something for my country."[22]

- *Show them what it takes to make an impact*

France-based English art critic John Berger (1926 – 2017) was a keen critic of global capitalism and particularly materialism. He maintained that the 'materialist

---

21   Carlopio, J. R., Andrewartha, G., & Armstrong, H. 2000.

22   Buechel, B., Cordon, C. & Kralik, M. 2013.

fantasy' robbed people of their spiritual power to respond to events with goodness. It turns out, he had a point: In a recent Singapore survey, seven out of 10 respondents managed to identify the top local brands of bubble tea. Only three in 10 could give correct answers to questions about native wildlife species.[23] This is yet another illustration of the fact that the age of consumerism is characterized by a compulsive search for new future sensations coupled with rampant forgetfulness.

Since the dawn of mass production and modern marketing, impressionable youngsters have been conditioned to indulge in transient tastes in fashion, music, food, fitness, anything: What matters is that this year's 'latest' hits and sensations will make way for new ones next year, and both will have been big sellers. Prescient, avant-garde French philosopher Guy Debord (1931 – 1994) in his 1967 book The Society of the Spectacle described it thus: "An all-enveloping and energy-draining spectacle that remains constant in terms of the amount of social space it occupies, while regularly changing its plastic, visual and verbal forms…a spectacle that for all its omnipresence in the minds of the populace, often has only a very tenuous relationship the empirical material reality of their day-to-day lives."[24]

To subscribe to values – social, political, environmental, community-oriented – is wonderful. But upholding, living those values calls for sacrifices and perseverance. It requires a detachment from self-interest and from an individual's temporal and self-absorbed perspective. It rests on the integrity of someone who can acknowledge that we cannot objectively discern facts from our fragmented and incomplete understanding. That in reality, nothing worthwhile is achieved without deep thought and hard work.

To participate is one thing; to exert influence is quite another. Too many young people opt out of even participating and prefer to remain on the fringes of social

---

23   Low, Y. 2020.

24   Debord, G., 1992.

and political action. To quote a 22-year-old first-year university undergraduate living in a metropolis in Asia: "I knew very little about actual policies and Members of Parliament, because it never seemed like the discussions in Parliament were affecting me, and I never had a say anyway."[25]

Information that has been centralized in the hands of a few tech giants and media groups will inevitably lead to impoverished public debate. It will also make it difficult for civil society and informal groupings to engage with their target audience. Action is always the answer. These days, cute hashtags don't cut it any more as 'activism'. You can use social media for activism – but your online presence should be matched with concrete actions, donations, and other measurable commitments to the social cause you support.[26] In the absence of action, people are easily swayed by dangerous, totalitarian arguments, developing an impression that nothing needs to be actually done to bring about a new world apart from destroying the old one.

- *Nurture empathy by providing exposure*

Empathy – even in the workplace, especially towards customers, is a word that has been bandied about vigorously in the past few years. At the same time, empathy is impossible to mandate. It's either there or it isn't. People are either predisposed to feel for others or they are not. With young people, what we can do is show them how other people live. Often these people – foreign workers, the homeless, the disabled, illegal immigrants – live a precarious existence in the same community as an affluent majority and yet – or perhaps inevitably – they are invisible.

Exposure can also take the simple form of sharing experiences with one's peers – especially those who live outside one's own comfortable social bubble.

---

25   todayonline.com

26   Reid, A. and Sehl, K. 2020.

For instance, Singapore's Today newspaper has run a column titled Gen Y Speaks. And its weekly content has nothing to do with the customary youthful preoccupations of entertainment, online dating or de-boxing one's latest purchase. The articles cover hard-hitting topics such as: 'What I am doing to tackle the menace of online sexual groomers'; 'What I learnt helping a friend cope with depression'; 'Having a single mother helped me grow up fast.'

- *Provide cognitive and actionable 'handles'*

Young people are not keen on structure; understandably they find it constraining. But real change is seldom achieved through a chaotic free-for-all. In recent years, grassroots movements like Occupy Wall Street managed to grab headlines but ultimately went down in history as a dud.

The Conservation Sentiments Survey, released in Singapore in October 2020, found that those aged 16 to 24 were more than twice as likely to support nature conservation efforts than older generations. The main barrier to playing a bigger part in this effort: According to 61% of respondents in this age bracket, they don't know where to begin. The upshot of the story: Young people support social causes; they want to see impact; but to guide them into actual opportunities like volunteering, physical (rather than media) avenues must be explored. They will no doubt be pleased with the experience and the result, but the first step will likely have to come from outside.[27]

- *Safeguard against a memory-less society*

As a blog reader commented recently: "The currency that we use to pay for the electronic spectacle is our attention, and in such hyper-mediated times as these, the charges mount up exponentially, until we find ourselves saddled with soul-crushing denial and disconnection."

———

27   Low, Y. 2020.

French anthropologist Lévi-Strauss talked about 'floating' or 'empty' signifiers — emotionally evocative terms presented without the contextual armature we need to imbue them with any stable and unequivocal semantic value.[28]

When the internet came along in the 1990s, we were often told, 'the medium is the message.' Today, the media – especially electronic media – is so much more than the message. The experience, the clickbait, the ritual behind viewing media content are always more powerful than the actual content and messaging it conveys. (In truth, the content is, in a case of 'context of no context', instantly displaced and forgotten anyway. Can you recall what you were looking at and/or reading online yesterday, two days ago, a week ago?...).

Then there is the ubiquitous appearance and opinion of celebrities who don't shy away from giving opinions on climate change, migration and genetic research. A quick and entertaining 10 minutes – or at a maximum, a TED talk – is the most demanding format there is. Having grown up with mobile devices and access to real-time information, millennials expect fast responses and fast outcomes. When reaching out to a customer service through social media, or when posting a query via text messaging, they expect quick replies. By the same token, often their instinct is to go for the result without the process.

Increasingly, nearly all headlines, articles and speeches are expected to be 'disruptive' – a thunderbolt from heaven, so to speak, that is guaranteed to knock the audience off their feet.

Luckily, and obviously, to quote from Robertson Davies's (1913 – 1995) novel The Rebel Angels (1981), the world couldn't stand so many thunderbolts. (Neither could the audience). But if we want to help today's youth appreciate that a lot of social media content is just that – a mirage; a consensus reality which is here this minute, gone the next, and wasn't necessarily 'real' to begin with – we need to insert some useful filters into the process of media consumption.

———

28   Mehlman, J., 1972.

Brain Pickings

In a world of Snapchat, Instagram and TikTok, US-based Bulgarian writer and blogger Maria Popova's Brain Pickings site (tagline: An inventory of the meaningful life) refers the readers of her inspirational articles not to online links but to actual paper books, available from a public library near you. Since 2006, her ads-free blog, focusing on off-the-beaten-path literary and arts commentary alongside cultural criticism, has been attracting a readership of several million every month.

Social media can be innovative and nurturing of talent

When channeled towards specific, practical objectives – and not just showing off one's 'perfect life' – social media has the power to mobilize powerful resources and deliver valuable, considered insight. It takes more than a few clicks and the results won't be instantaneous. But the process will take days rather than weeks or months as conventional surveys and similar marketing projects usually do.

Think and organize beyond metrics and numbers

The motto of Domestic Data Streamers, a creative studio from Barcelona that has been on a mission to trigger change using data, storytelling and design, is: "The world cannot be understood without numbers, but it will not be understood with numbers alone. Any meaningful interchange of information between people needs to carry emotions, experiences and create knowledge."

In segments like consumer goods, working with real data and fast testing allows specialists to test and iterate ideas such as logos and website designs with up to 20,000 social media users and within 48 hours. Thus, the outcome is shaped in real time, through live market input, and takes out the guesswork and weeks of meetings on top of much of the cost.

- *Stimulate Expansiveness – Inspiration – Expression*

Did Michelangelo ever see in nature what he afterwards created in his art? Did he and other great artists of Italian Renaissance simply capture what they saw in the outside world? Copy and paste? No, they were perfectionists who were possessed of an unusual degree of mental and spiritual expansiveness. By giving room to this expansiveness and exercising it, they drew inspiration (from the Latin spirare = breathe; thus the literal meaning of inspire is to fill the heart/mind with something exciting[29]). Finally, they released this inspiration through the channel of artistic expression.

Can we emulate the masters? We can, if we give our minds the time and the space to become humbled and liberated in our outlook; to breathe, absorb and express. In return, the mind will lead us to new ways of thinking, sensing and imagining. To quote Italo Calvino's (1923 – 1985) Six Memos for the Next Millennium (1988): …I have to change my approach, look at the world from a different perspective, with a different logic and with fresh methods of cognition and verification. The images of lightness that I seek should not fade away like dreams dissolved by the realities of present and future…[30]

Young values in a post-Covid world

The recipe that Robert Musil put forward amid his own turn-of-the-century, end-of-the-[Austro-Hungarian]-empire and WWI crises – of accepting science and reason while underpinning them with social and individual values – is just as valid today. Musil was preoccupied with how society organizes ideas about life. He was also concerned with what he saw as young people's aura of 'keenly analytical passivity' – of a search for meaning that turned into indifference, having been repeatedly dashed by life's deep ambiguities. As he pointed out

---

29   etymonline.com

30   Calvino, I., 1988.

in his unfinished novel The Man Without Qualities: "Even in his greatest dedication to science he had never managed to forget that people's goodness and beauty come from what they believe, not from what they know."[31]

As at the end of 2020, more and more young people have realized that there is only that much Instagram-scrolling and Netflix binge-watching one can enjoy on any given day. Some have turned to volunteering – raising money to buy food for foreign workers – some of them jobless because of the Covid-related downturn yet not allowed to travel to their home countries; donating second-hand laptops to students who needed them to make the most of home-based learning; volunteering to give free tuition online; congregating on Zoom to help friends update their resumes and prep for upcoming job interviews. Many are eager to help offset their parents' lost income and determined to 'grab any opportunity that comes my way'.

---

31   Musil, R., 2015.

Chapter 6

Revitalizing ambition and faith in the future

"Live the questions now. Perhaps you will then gradually, without noticing it, live along some distant day into the answer."

Rainer Maria Rilke (1875–1926), in a letter to his protégé, 19-year-old poet Franz Xaver Kappus

Ours is the age of purpose

The new millennium has revived debates on business as a deeply social place where humans not only create economic value but also interact, overcome obstacles, learn from each other, derive meanings from everyday situations, and try to make a difference. Traditional paradigms of economics have cast entrepreneurs in the role of rationalistic agents whose only objective is maximizing profit and shareholder value. Nonetheless, aiming to find a sense of purpose has always been a key underpinning of human psychology: It is a fundamentally human need to see tangible outcomes of one's work, to make an impact on the team, the company, the customer as well as the community and society. Purpose transcends the self and connects it to something larger than the self. Thus, business interests necessarily intersect with a higher, authentic purpose.

As far back as the 1990s, visions of business were put forward which argued that effective management requires stepping outside the mechanistic, 'life as a machine' paradigm of organization, strategy and business, and injecting the conduct of business with a sense of common purpose.[1] In recent years, these concepts have acquired new urgency: Social commentators have pointed out that many of today's socioeconomic problems are a direct manifestation of business that has been divorced from society, community and the environment. Growing interest in sustainability and stewardship has led to reevaluations of the long-standing view of humans as self-serving, rational choice-making Homo economicus. Meanwhile, the rise of robotics, machine learning and artificial intelligence has brought into focus the value of human-centricity in organizations and business.

As a result, more and more companies seek to frame their main business in ways that provide a sense of meaning beyond generating profits. However, unlike financial indicators, purpose is largely intangible[2] and therefore elusive. In many cases, its presence is indicated by proxies – for instance, when a company is rated as a 'great place to work.' A sense of purpose is what shapes people's beliefs and guides their actions, but it typically defies measuring or even visualizing.

Recent history, macro trends show us that development rooted in values is the only way forward

Economics has shown a growing recognition that inequality will adversely affect both growth and stability.[3] Yet up until the 2008 financial crisis, moral and ethical considerations were largely excluded from business education and theory. In his 2005 article Bad Management Theories are Destroying Good Management Practices, the late management scholar Sumantra Ghoshal (1948

---

1   Bartlett, C.A. and Ghoshal, S., 1994.

2   Gartenberg, C., Prat, A. and Serafeim, G., 2019.

3   Case, J. 2015.

– 2004) of London Business School argued that "by propagating ideologically inspired amoral theories, business schools have actively freed their students from any sense of moral responsibility".[4]

According to the chairman and former CEO of Nestlé Paul Bulcke, at the core of the 2008 global debt crisis was a values crisis in which: "Too many people and businesses had been seduced by or pressured into delivering on short-term egoistic targets and there was a general shift in thinking towards 'me-now' instead of 'us-tomorrow'. Leaders need to demonstrate their respect by going back to the basic role of business – value creation for society as a whole with a long-term perspective."

There is a growing understanding that business cannot operate independently of social, geopolitical, environmental, and human needs, and must indeed balance these diverse needs. The community cannot be just another stakeholder in business but is in fact the purpose of its existence. The companies that will thrive in the future can no longer be concerned only with their own demands, benefits, and financial returns. Business interests necessarily intersect with a higher, authentic purpose.

New business narratives emphasize the context in which companies operate; embrace stakeholder and community involvement; uphold economic as well as societal value; focus on wealth creation for all; and seek to make economic and social systems more equitable, more sustainable, and more inclusive. Many years ago, Henry Mintzberg (1939-) put forward the ideal of a manager who was committed to a specific company or industry, and not to management as a means of personal advancement.

Similarly, Sumantra Ghoshal spoke of management as "a calling and a profession that sits at the heart of creating good for society and for individuals". In his books A

---

4   Ghoshal, S., 2005.

New Manifesto for Management (1999) and Sumantra Ghoshal on Management: A Force for Good (2005), he encouraged managers to move past narrow economic assumptions and recognize society as an organizational economy rather than a market economy.[5][6] His writings combined management theory with pragmatism, reflecting the emphasis he placed on spending time with corporate managers and directly engaging with the practice of management.

Today, a number of proposed new models of growth are competing for policymakers' and economists' attention. What they share is the vision of development that is rooted in values and in social and environment impact on top of economic impact. The table below summarizes some of these value-based approaches.

Table: Value-based approaches - a quick synopsis

Concept	Main tenets	Proponents
Inclusive prosperity	• Major sources of inequality derive from capital rather than labor. • Inequality is detrimental to growth. It is a source of economic and social instability. • Governments would do well to tax wealth in addition to income.	Thomas Piketty, Joseph Stiglitz, Paul Krugman, Daron Acemoglu

Table continued on next page

---

5   Ghoshal, S., Bartlett, C.A. and Moran, P., 1999.

6   Ghoshal, S., 2005.

Table continued from previous page

| Inclusive business | • Inclusive business is a business approach to development.

• Cross-domain collaborations between companies, investors, NGOs and other players are needed to embed purpose in business.

• Imagine the transformation in the world economy if every citizen on the planet had access to financial services.

• The 'base of the pyramid' – that mass market of low-income consumers in developing societies such as South Asia and Africa – can be a source of not only business opportunity (by integrating these segments into business models and value chains) but also next practices in development, digital entrepreneurship and social innovation.

• Building on existing traditions and practices of solidarity and self-help. | GSK, Unilever, Visa, Business Fights Poverty |

Table continued on next page

Table continued from previous page

Economics of mutuality	• Recognizing natural capital, human capital, and social capital alongside financial capital. • Developing profitable solutions to the problems in a company's entire ecosystem. • Finding the right level of profitability that will maximize a company's performance. • Pioneer ways to combine technology and sustainability to solve global problems.	Enterprise for Society Center (E4S), elea Center for Social Innovation, Economics of Mutuality
Corporate stewardship	• Overcoming agency theory to take a broader stakeholder view. • Businesses as trustees of human, social, natural assets. • Enhancing the quality of these assets over time. • Focus on long-term time frames and outcomes of ownership and management.	David Schoorman, Lex Donaldson, Sumantra Ghoshal, Henry Mintzberg, Stewardship Asia Centre

Table continued on next page

Table continued from previous page

Council for Inclusive Capitalism	• Set up a coalition of large investors, companies, unions and foundations to create a more equitable and trusted economic system. • Make capitalism less socially and environmentally damaging by building a fair, trustworthy economic system that could address humanity's biggest challenges. • Return economics and finance to an ethical approach which favors humans. • Reassert the central place of humans in social and economic life.	Pope Francis, Lynn Forester de Rothschild, Mastercard, Dupont, Salesforce
Doughnut economics	• Combining the concept of planetary boundaries with the complementary concept of social boundaries.	Kate Raworth
Green New Deal	• Addressing in concert the issues of climate change and economic inequality.	Ann Pettifor, Naomi Klein
Economics of belonging	• Re-examining the role of economics in today's widening inequality.	Martin Sandbu

In sketching out new models of growth, it is also useful to revisit some of the older models. They may have remained confined to academic journals, but perhaps that is because the ideas behind them were simply ahead of their time. Let's face it – inclusive, responsible, human-centric capitalism wasn't invented in 2020. As with all domains of knowledge, it is anchored in social thought that was put forward decades ago. Thus for instance E. F. Schumacher's (1911 – 1977) Small is Beautiful. Economics as if People Mattered was first published in 1973.[7] Sustainable development, the finite character of natural resources, passive building designs, people-centered technology – all of these subjects sound as topical and relevant – if not more so – today as they did when Schumacher penned his essays 50 years ago.

Pope Francis's involvement in the Council for Inclusive Capitalism has raised eyebrows in some quarters. In reality, the modern-day Church has long been a keen observer of the world of work and the way it shapes the lives of billions around the world. Pope Leo XIII's 1891 encyclical Rerum novarum (of revolutionary change in the world) is also known as Rights and Duties of Capital and Labor. It addresses the largely harrowing conditions of the working classes as well as the relationship between capital and workers and between government and citizens.

Other religions have cultivated their own bodies of knowledge regarding business, business ethics, economics and social justice. Islamic investing, a branch of socially responsible investments, has grown into a trillion-dollar global market. Islamic financial practices avoid the practice of usury and financial speculation ('making money with money'). They favor financial instruments which are backed by tangible assets. Meanwhile, Buddhist societies have seen calls for articulating Buddhist economics that would endorse their collectivist cultures as well as developmental objectives. Prioritizing the maximization of profit and placing material goods ahead of people should have no place in such an economic system.

---

7   Schumacher, E.F., 1978.

To change course, we need to acknowledge today's skepticism and pessimism

Some historians believe that a civilization's collapse is typically preceded by a deep sense of moral and ethical crisis in young people. In his 1976 book The Fall of Empires, John Glubb (1897 – 1986) compared 13 different empires throughout human history. He found that widespread pessimism, cynicism and a cult of celebrity (i.e. worship of fake 'idols' over deities) was a consistent predictor of a looming downfall.

Back in the 1970s, 'life in the year 2000' was a popular comic strip theme. It revolved around a prosperous, leisure society where work has been automated, a family bungalow could be assembled in a day and weekend trips to the Moon were as commonplace as a bike ride to the grocery store. Looking around today, we have to acknowledge that the system has fed a sense of alienation and diminishing prospects for many young people. Technology has overtaken the human capacity to absorb and utilize it, and yet it has largely failed to eradicate the socioeconomic issues it promised to tackle with such gusto just 15-20 years ago. The result has been the contemporary citizenry's habituation to screens, accompanied for many by an acute sense of precarity and desperation. Those who control the screens control the world.

At present, millennials are more dissatisfied with democracy than any previous generation at the same stage in life. The report from Cambridge University's Centre for the Future of Democracy – which combined data from over 4.8 million respondents from 160 countries between 1973 and 2020 – found that globally, younger generations are less satisfied with democracy than previous cohorts at the same age. This is the first generation in living memory to have a global majority who are disillusioned with the way democracy works while in their twenties and thirties. The growing intergenerational divide is blamed in part on economic exclusion. Higher debt burdens, lower odds of owning a home, greater challenges in starting a family, and reliance upon inherited wealth rather than hard work and talent to succeed are all contributors to youth discontent.[8] When people feel trapped and patronized by progress, then any alternative – even regress – will feel like freedom.[9]

What is clear is that in the past few years, the limitations of capitalism and globalization have come into full view.[10] [11] Sure, the idea (a futuristic one, or so it seemed at the time) that growth cannot go on unchecked forever has been on the table for the past 50 years.[12] [13] But the world was too busy casting off painful legacies of the 20th century to entertain the concept. Today, despite decades of growth, income inequalities among and also within countries continue to rise in many parts of the world.[14] At the time of writing this book, the global health crisis of 2020 has shown how vulnerable the world economy is, not only in terms of growth but also in public debt, employment and people's wellbeing: Global government debt has already reached its highest level in peacetime.[15] Worldwide poverty is expected to go up for the first time in 30 years.[16] As developing countries witness a capital flight, Africa is entering its first recession in 25 years.[17] The pandemic has been a boon for online learning, yet in sub-Saharan Africa, 89% of students don't have a home computer while 82% lack internet access.[18] The statistics are sobering.

———

8   Tidey, A. 2020.

9   Davies, W. 2018.

10   Minsky, H.P., 1994.

11   Cohen, T., 2012.

12   Meadows, D.H., Meadows, D.L., Randers, J. and Behrens, W.W., 1972.

13   Meadows, D., Randers, J. and Meadows, D., 2004.

14   sustainabledevelopment.un.org

15   Stubbington, T. 2019.

16   wider.unu.edu

17   Mwenda, M. 2021.

18   en.unesco.org

For all the talk of sustainability, looking around in 2020, many social commentators have shifted their focus to what they see as a chronic sense of unsustainability.[19] Categories like 'post-growth', 'post-capitalism', 'post-consumerism', just a few years ago the domain of radical doomsayers, are flooding into the mainstream. TV shows such as the History Channel's 2009 Life After People suddenly feel like an eerie prediction rather than an innocent piece of sci-fi entertainment. Through it all, the perception is firming up that technological progress, which makes economic growth possible, does not satisfy the fundamental needs of man and is used above all to maintain and strengthen the system.[20] Technology can improve or undermine democracy depending on how it is used and who controls it. At present, it sometimes seems controlled by few. History knows that when a great deal of power is concentrated in the hands of a few, the outcome is not good for the many, not good for democracy.[21]

Having faith in the future is the best way to make it better

History – and classical literature – show that disillusionment often comes from a lack of opportunity to apply one's capabilities, rather than from economic stagnation. Russian literature of the first half of the 19th century presents a bevy of characters – affluent and aristocratic – who in spite of their education and intellect perceive themselves as superfluous, 'unnecessary.' From Pushkin's Eugene Onegin to Goncharov's Oblomov, the outside world has no demand for their skills, is uninterested in innovations and offers them no avenue for meaningful action. Their stories may be romantic in an 'us against the world' way but come without a happily-ever-after.

---

19   Blühdorn, I., 2017.

20   Willener, A. ed., 2013.

21   Anderson, J. and Rainie, L. 2020.

In the 2020s, we cannot afford to let young people's talent and passion go to waste. Based on this book's findings and observations, we want to propose the following actions and next practices:

- *We need new data – but it is a different kind of data*

In the previous chapters we described the vibrant emerging landscape of innovation and talent. This landscape is dotted with smart cities, open innovation clusters, coworking spaces and other players. As such, virtually all of them fly under the radar of 'official' statistic and data collection exercises, whose focus is on top-level, national metrics such as GDP. As John Maynard Keynes (1883 – 1946) said. "The difficulty lies not so much in developing new ideas as in escaping from old ones." Additionally, we showed that around the world, the new quality of organizing – in education, work, innovation, customer-centricity – draws on attributes including caring, empathy, and expression. The old, impersonal metrics whose bedrock is GDP give us very little grip on this agile, flexible, re-humanized economy. What we truly want to measure – at organizational, city and other subnational levels – are indicators like happiness, optimism and employee engagement.

Using data for empowerment rather than surveillance and control is also the focus of Sarah Williams's 2020 book Data Action: Using Data for Public Good (MIT Press). Through a mix of historical framing, critical reflection and instruction, it demonstrates how collaborative, methodologically pluralistic, reflective, and publicly responsive modes of data design can incite civic change. It provides a guide for working with data in more ethical and responsible ways, emphasizing collaboration among data scientists, policy experts, data designers, and the public.[22]

---

22   Williams, S., 2020.

- *Connect history with today's young people's own impressions and experiences*

The emergency surrounding Covid-19 has been a rude awakening for the young generation, accustomed to frequent travel and a flexible lifestyle. But it has also served up a reminder that crises and cataclysms occur in every generation. The last 20 years alone saw 9/11, SARS and a global financial crisis, and people – including young people – had to overcome and cope with the aftermath of each of those events.

If these post-2000 events are largely forgotten by many, what about the history of the past few hundred years? How reliable is our modern historical perspective in this digital era of real-time everything where cultural amnesia is actively encouraged? Was yesterday really better than today's reality? Cognitive scientist Steven Pinker's 2018 book Enlightenment Now: The Case for Reason, Science, Humanism, and Progress uses social science data to show a general improvement of the human condition over recent history. In fact, the book's message could be summarized as 'now is the best time to be alive.'[23] Its main impact may be elsewhere, however: Defending scientific rationality and liberal humanism with quantitative data on health, wealth, inequality, the environment, peace and democracy, the book offers proof that, often, the best way to settle an argument is by measuring and comparing specific indicators. Relying on measurable facts may well be our best – and yet so frequently overlooked – weapon against tribalism, political populism and the media's every-increasing dose of doom and gloom.

Most experts in anger management techniques encourage us to reframe the unsettling experience we are going through. Will today's events appear and feel as disorienting six months from now as they do in this moment? Unlikely. The more we adjust our sights to take in a longer view, the more measured and reasoned our response will be. The same applies to our view of the present –

---

23   Pinker, S., 2018.

with all its snags, traps and dilemmas – in its historical context. Those who are conscious of history will better appreciate the nature of long-term change. There are areas where we are failing, clearly. But there are also those where we have done well – so well, in fact, that the outcomes are taken for granted. We must also appreciate our collective historical wisdom as societies: The reason that today's habits, beliefs and traditions are still with us is probably because, for centuries, they have served a purpose and helped us make sense of the world around us.

Viewed through that prism, we may be inspired to learn more, for example, about the Roman Empire on whose foundations the western world continues to rest today. It was the Roman entity that bequeathed to us such social fundamentals as the republic, the legal system, public order, peace, security and modern infrastructure. One of the sources of the empire's greatness was its employment of meticulous land surveyors and geometrists who not only practiced but also formalized their techniques, which as a result remained unsurpassed until the end of the 18th century. Emperor Augustus (63 BC – AD 14) instituted a survey of the entire 'Orbis Romanus' (Roman world), in order that each taxpayer should know exactly his resources and obligations. The results of this survey were tabulated by the author Hyrummetricus.[24]

Keep cool and think clearly

The late Roman Empire also gave us the philosophy of stoicism, best captured in emperor Marcus Aurelius's (121-180) diary called Meditations or To Myself. A slim and highly readable volume of thought on life, time, friendship, ethics, self-improvement, what is or isn't real

Box continued on next page

---

24   fig.net

Box continued from previous page

and other timeless subjects, it remains popular to this day. Stoicism was built on the foundation of rationality, promoting rational thought as the main conduit to achieving things outside the self. The stoics took pride in the systematic nature of their philosophy. They also encouraged self-mastery, tranquility of mind and participation in human affairs. Crucially, the stoics saw their philosophy as not just theory but a way of life.[25] Today's fans of stoicism firmly believe that the philosophy has made them happier, wiser and more resilient, and overall better people, parents and professionals. They consider stoic thought to contain some of the greatest wisdom in the history of the world.[26]

For Marcus Aurelius himself, stoic philosophy was a source of calm in the middle of a storm. To quote from his diary: "To bear in mind constantly that all of this has happened before... And will happen again—the same plot from beginning to end... Only the people differ."[27]

His 20-year reign was marked by the rise of Christianity which would eventually eclipse Greek and Roman beliefs; a plague epidemic that left an estimated 7 to 8 million of the empire's residents dead; and wars with 'barbarians at the gates' – foreign tribes encroaching on the northern border. It was during military campaigns – according to the opening chapter, "among the [barbarian tribe of] Quadi on the river Gran [Hron in today's Slovakia]" that Marcus started writing Meditations.

• *Engage with tangible, underutilized microcosms of the future such as coworking centers*

When hearing of digital nomads and coworking locations, most people picture a bunch of adolescents lounging in hammocks. In reality, these facilities are

---

25   plato.stanford.edu

26   dailystoic.com

27   Aurelius, M., 2013.

replete with progressive social, communication, work, business and travel practices. Digital nomads think deeply about community, impact, climate, social justice. They experiment with and put in practice a number of social movements, from less-waste lifestyles to 'conscious consumerism.'

Partnering with digital nomads to address issues of depopulation in Southeastern Europe

UNDP Serbia's Accelerator Lab became interested in digital nomads because the UNDP team was working on understanding the topic of depopulation in Serbia.

Depopulation is a global issue affecting a range of countries, some aspects of which are low birth rate, high emigration and no immigration. As a complex and multidimensional challenge, it can't be addressed with a single solution.

Conversely, Serbia is a country attractive to digital nomads.

The lifestyle of digital nomads is seen as reflective of current and coming trends. By seeing who they are and what they do, UNDP sought to encourage them to stay in Serbia longer. The hypothesis was that if they can manage this, the results can be applied to other freelancers or IT professionals in Serbian diaspora to help stop brain drain.

Together with the Digital Serbia Initiative, UNDP analyzed digital professionals from abroad who have decided to live and work in Belgrade. By attracting a digital workforce, Serbia might be able to tackle the problem of skilled emigration. In the first half of 2020, Nomad List ranked Belgrade as Europe's no. 7 destination for digital nomads.

UNDP's Digital Nomad Scanner then examined foreign digital workers in Belgrade, and what their 'user journey' is. Who are they, and why do they prefer this lifestyle? What are the most important factors in choosing a place for temporarily living and working?

Box continued on next page

Box continued from previous page

Based on the survey, the average digital nomad who visits Serbia is a 34-year-old man from North America, travelling alone. They are entrepreneurs in IT who know about Serbia from personal connections.

They consider a dependable internet connection and low living expenses, as well as culture, climate, the state of civil liberties, transportation, language, air quality and how long it takes to reach the beaches or mountains.

Belgrade as 'Europe outside of the EU' is particularly attractive because it has the vibe of a world-class metropolis, while being one of the cheapest and most accessible European capitals.

As for working, there are more than ten coworking spaces, and many work-friendly bars and cafes. These 'working infrastructure' elements are crucial for location-independent digital professionals.

There is external recognition of the booming tech scene and startup ecosystem, with more and more major global startup companies emerging from Serbia. Per Startup Genome assessment, the Belgrade and Novi Sad ecosystems are seeing particularly noteworthy success in gaming and blockchain technology. The BBC ranked Belgrade as one of the most creative cities in the world, and Lonely Planet called it "outspoken, adventurous, proud and audacious."

Positioning Belgrade as a city that understands the needs of digital nomads would infuse much-needed skills. Digital nomads bring with them new knowledge and experiences, thus enriching the technological scene and giving it an international character.[28]

---

28   undp.medium.com

- *Designing a new social contract*

What the above paradigms have shown us is that 21st-century economists are embracing complexity and evolutionary thinking. They live in a time where they have a wealth of data at their disposal, as well as a growing body of digital tools and techniques. In addition, the Covid crisis has inspired and emboldened many to bring new approaches to evaluating how the economic order that shapes society has come to be the way it is today. In the words of Thomas Piketty: "Economic ideologies are very fragile, and times of crisis are always times when dominant ideologies are being challenged and possibly go through major transformations."[29] According to Piketty, unless societies can shine the spotlight on their inequalities and justify them, their whole political and social project is in danger of collapse.[30]

Economists and econometrists are now better equipped than ever before to diagnose the system; expose its inner contradictions; accurately identify and also predict consequences; and come up with proposals for new practices and behaviors at policy, investment, business management and social levels. Crucially, they can create real solutions based on facts and metrics. Increasingly, these solutions consider business as taking place in a social context. The young generation, if properly engaged and steered, will fuel vibrant new trends in values-based social, economic, political and technological development.

Applying this stakeholder approach to the issues facing the young generation, we can directly ask young people about their perceptions, expectations and aspirations; about what it is they truly hope to receive and achieve in school, employment, interactions with government agencies but also on social media and other digital platforms. With today's technology, we have an unprecedent opportunity to do so not only comprehensively, across large and representative samples of respondents and with precision, but also at great speed and minimum cost. Quite literally, the information and insight we seek is there for the asking.

---

29   Norbrook, N. 2020.

30   Kahloon, I. 2020.

- *From MDGs to SDGs*

So much has been written about the UN's SDGs, adopted in 2015, it may give young people in particular the impression that the SDGs were simply 'declared' by the global body that is the UN, once and for all. In reality, the 17 goals and 169 related targets that make up the SDGs are the result of the biggest consultation in UN history, a process that involved 83 national surveys and engaged over 7 million people over three years.[31] Coupled with that scale, the process was also more inclusive than ever, bringing together national governments as well as business, civil society, higher education and citizens.

The SDGs are testimony to how the world had changed in just a few years, since the 2000 introduction of the Millennium Development Goals (MDGs), which targeted developing countries. The MDGs included the following goals: 1) Eradicate extreme poverty and hunger; 2) Achieve universal primary education; 3) Promote gender equality and empower women; 4) Reduce child mortality; 5) Improve maternal health; 6) Combat HIV/AIDs, malaria, and other diseases; 7) Ensure environmental sustainability; and 8) Develop a global partnership for development.[32]

SDGs give individual countries the freedom to set up their own national frameworks for how they plan to achieve the goals. Just as the business world has in recent years stepped outside the traditional silos and embraced cross-functional, cross-disciplinary teams as the best vehicles for innovative product development and tackling customers' problems and pain points, SDG strategies encourage thinking across different sectors and across institutional boundaries.[33] Thus for example the International Telecommunication Union (ITU) and UNESCO jointly launched the Broadband Commission for Digital Development. In education, the UN Global Compact formulated a set of

---

31   inclusivebusiness.net

32   sdgfund.org

33   undp.org

Principles for Responsible Management Education (PRME) which champion responsible management education, research and thought-leadership globally. Collaboration is key to navigating an uncertain and intricate future. Working with a diverse range of partners, who bring different expertise and perspectives to the table, opens up new opportunities and solutions. Previously edgy and alternative tools like crowdsourcing have now gone mainstream even in formal settings like higher education. It also becomes important to ensure that the benefits are shared among partners to embed sustainability.

The 17 SDGs include these goals: 1) End poverty in all its forms everywhere; 2) End hunger, achieve food security and improved nutrition, and promote sustainable agriculture; 3) Ensure healthy lives and promote wellbeing for all at all ages; 4) Ensure inclusive and equitable quality education and promote lifelong learning opportunities for all; 5) Achieve gender equality and empower all women and girls; 6) Ensure availability and sustainable management of water and sanitation for all; 7) Ensure access to affordable, reliable, sustainable, and modern energy for all; 8) Promote sustained, inclusive and sustainable economic growth, full and productive employment, and decent work for all; 9) Build resilient infrastructure, promote inclusive and sustainable industrialization, and foster innovation; 10) Reduce inequality within and among countries; 11) Make cities and human settlements inclusive, safe, resilient and sustainable; 12) Ensure sustainable consumption and production patterns; 13) Take urgent action to combat climate change and its impacts; 14) Conserve and sustainably use the oceans, seas, and marine resources for sustainable development; 15) Protect, restore and promote sustainable use of terrestrial ecosystems, sustainably manage forests, combat desertification, halt and reverse land degradation, and halt biodiversity loss; 16) Promote peaceful and inclusive societies for sustainable development, provide access to justice for all, and build effective, accountable and inclusive institutions at all levels; and 17) Strengthen the means of implementation and revitalize the global partnership for sustainable development.[34]

---

34   sdgfund.org

Building on the momentum achieved by the MDGs, each of the SDGs comes with a clear measurement/monitoring mechanism. The SDGs include ICT-specific targets in four of the 17 goals, particularly with regard to SDG 4 on Quality Education (target 4b), SDG 5 on Gender Equality (target 5b), SDG 9 on Industry, Innovation and Infrastructure (target 9c) and SDG 17 on Partnerships for the Goals (target 17.8). There are at least 38 other targets that rely on universal and affordable access to ICT and broadband to reach achievement, including science and technology targets and references to internet, infrastructure, innovation, information access, increased efficiency, early warning, disaster risk management, knowledge sharing, and data. In fact, when announcing the SDGs, the UN called for a data revolution for sustainable development. It followed up by rolling out several other initiatives and working groups on data issues.

We need new ways of measuring – but also thinking and knowing

The SDGs are a child of our age of complexity. To achieve them will take not only rigorous metrics and their tracking but also new ways of thinking. Among these, there is a growing demand in most organizations for cognitive skills like sensemaking and systems thinking. Stimulating curiosity and continuous learning, sensemaking is about bringing together a diversity of perspectives in order to arrive at a consolidated understanding and then testing and refining it – or dismissing it if necessary. Sensemaking is about listening and digging for more data, identifying problems, asking lots of questions, and reflecting on what has been learned in the past. Systems thinking is a type of adaptive thinking allows leaders to visualize and anticipate the worlds of possibilities inside and outside the business. Once a largely theoretical concept in computer science, systems thinking has come alive to serve as a conduit to finding patterns in data and to spotting hitherto overlooked connections and relationships. Systems thinking offers a method for businesses to look at their activities, the needs of society and new opportunities as part of a whole ecosystem, rather than in isolation. This holistic approach can both support more purposeful and generally beneficial economic activity as well as uncover possibilities that may not have been obvious before.

Roadmaps for achieving the SDGs are increasingly calling for developing systems thinking and changemaking skills among students. That, of course is 'easier said than done' – unless we really engage students in co-designing and co-creating their own learning environments and opportunities for experiential learning related to SDG strategies and outcomes; and make real-world collaborative projects the core of young people's academic programs and school modules.

Conclusion

"If all the economists were laid end to end, they'd never reach a conclusion."

George Bernard Shaw

"Despair is the conclusion of fools."

Benjamin Disraeli

Where do we go from here?

Problems are rarely unique or unprecedented, and neither are solutions. Putting technology and talent to good use in a world of uncertainty and change has been a challenge that societies have faced since the dawn of recorded history. Despite personal loss and economic instability, people have continued to learn and to find applications for their knowledge. A quick peek at the biographies of some of the founders of scientific disciplines as we know them today will reveal that they never stopped learning and questioning, even during plague epidemics. It is a timely reminder of how strong and adaptable we humans are.

Similarly, the thinkers from 100 years ago described our own society's anxieties with almost unsettling accuracy. And the recipe they came to advocate, through much soul searching, remains just as valid today: The landscape will always be dotted with challenges. Accepting science and reason (as anchoring factors) while underpinning them with social and individual values is the best way to bridge many of the modern world's paradoxes and contradictions.

The chapters in this book have been our attempt to bring this message home and help operationalize it, by drawing readers' attention to the following themes:

- *The raw energy of good, pro-social intentions needs to be channeled in productive directions*

The 2020s have set about to reimagine the nature of work, education, and innovation. We propose that for this reimagining to be meaningful and fruitful, we need a sense of context, ideally informed by relevant, stimulating lessons from the past. We also need strong foundations and departure points to guide the process – i.e., tools and cognitive handles that will help us grasp patterns and developments.

The millennial generations have been passionate about infusing learning and work with meaning, connecting and people-centricity. Yet theirs also happens to be a hypermediated era of random access and instant everything, where most information is presented as revelation whose objective is to shock and 'influence' (typically in kneejerk, visceral, emotional ways) rather than educate or inspire. In this never-ending stream of digital content, filters have all but disappeared – and with them, the ability (or even necessity) to take a step back, examine and question the underlying assumptions, gain access to non-digital sources, or link observations and principles from one discipline to another.

- *Facts are the best ammunition to counter hype as well as skepticism*

Much of the insight that is at our fingertips about technology, innovation and talent has been packaged in 20 years' worth of global indices whose structure and key messages this book has described in some detail. In many of the central debates on the benefits of tech, innovation and talent, the body of knowledge that is captured in these publications has proven to be relevant and in fact prescient. It has steered clear of promoting tech and innovation for tech's and innovation's sake – and has instead consistently pinpointed, connected, and analyzed the driving forces of today's digital economy: Not just technology but the impact of technology; not only talent but talent & mobility; talent & cities; talent & the rollout of AI. The result is powerful, compelling guidance and benchmarks which have been customized for companies, government agencies, and citizens. Crucially, the indices have managed to stay away from mechanical box- and eyeball-counting. Instead, they have reaffirmed a perspective on technology, innovation and talent that can be summarized as 'it's not what or how many IT systems we have; it's what we do with them and how we use them to create impact for businesses, governments and societies.'

- *Metrics are critically important for understanding what is happening and correcting what is to be corrected*

Exponential growth in data; rise of data-driven decision making and indeed entire organizational cultures; adoption of virtual collaborative platforms that can swiftly mobilize ideas and perspectives from a global talent pool; proliferation of AI systems; rapid adaptability as the new source of competitive strength: All of these trends that are becoming synonymous with the 2020s need to be consistently measured – both as a way out of drowning in the rapidly growing volumes of data; and as an instrument of connecting the past with the present and the future.

The corporate dictum of 'what gets measured gets done' is a child of 20th-century management. As a result, it does metrics a bit of disservice by essentially painting them as a mechanism of control. In reality, measuring trends and developments increasingly opens the door to a wealth of perspectives that directly translate into new configurations and opportunities.

With the right tools and perspectives, we can set our minds to the bigger issues:

Trust and confidence in the future will directly feed into young people's ambition

In order to tackle today's global challenges as reflected in the SDGs, we – managers, workers, policymakers, students, social activists – truly need to give the best of ourselves. A more open world, where inequalities are shrinking rather than growing, is a big part of the ambition that the younger generation can claim as its own.

Where do we want to go?

Today's young generation has an 'embarrassment of riches' at their fingertips: Knowledge, technology, imagination as well as innovation which increasingly includes AI-enhanced 'superpowers'. Importantly, they have values – a nurturing presence of human spirit that thrives on caring, compassion and social impact. If the rest of society can help the youth activate its ambition and enthusiasm, the outcomes may well be impossible to beat. In addition, we need to be acutely aware of where young talent has been gravitating and concentrating; what issues (economic but also psychological and existential ones) it has been grappling with; and which players are in the best position to attract and develop that talent.

References

Chapter 2 — Do self-driving cars need rear-view mirrors?

1. quoteinvestigator.com/2012/12/06/future-not-used

2. Aurelius, M., 2013. Marcus Aurelius: Meditations, Books 1-6. Oxford University Press.

3. Bauman, Z., 2007. Liquid times: Living in an age of uncertainty. Cambridge: Polity.

4. Vico, G., 1725. Principi di una scienza nuova intorno alla natura delle nazioni per la quale si ritruovano i principi di altro sistema (Principles of a New Science Concerning the Nature of Nations, through Which Are Recovered the Principles of Another System of the Natural Law of the People). Mosca.

5. Harper, K., 2017. The fate of Rome: Climate, disease, and the end of an empire. Princeton University Press.

6. Strickland, A. (2019). Why a volcanic eruption caused a 'year without a summer' in 1816. [online] CNN. Available at: edition.cnn.com/2019/09/17/world/tambora-eruption-year-without-summer-scn/index.html [Accessed 2 Apr. 2021].

7. Gunderman, R. (2016). How a volcano in Indonesia led to the creation of Frankenstein. [online] The Conversation. Available at: theconversation.com/how-a-volcano-in-indonesia-led-to-the-creation-of-frankenstein-65293 [Accessed 2 Apr. 2021].

8. Hazael, V. (2017). 200 years since the father of the bicycle Baron Karl von Drais invented the 'running machine' | Cycling UK. [online] We Are Cycling UK. Available at: cyclinguk.org/cycle/draisienne-1817-2017-200-years-cycling-innovation-design [Accessed 2 Apr. 2021].

9. Patty, W.L. and Johnson, L.S., 1953. The adjustments of personality.

10. Spengler, O., 1991. The decline of the West. Oxford University Press, USA.

11. Piketty, T., 2015. About capital in the twenty-first century. American Economic Review, 105(5), pp.48-53.

12. britannica.com/topic/millennialism/Millennialism-from-the-Renaissance-to-the-modern-world

13. Cohn, N., 2011. The pursuit of the millennium: Revolutionary millenarians and mystical anarchists of the middle ages. Random House.

14. Williams, C.C., 2005. A commodified world?: Mapping the limits of capitalism. Zed Books.

15. Fukuyama, F., 2006. The end of history and the last man. Simon and Schuster.

16. Krugman, P.R., 1997. Development, geography, and economic theory (Vol. 6). MIT press.

17. Blühdorn, I., 2017. Post-capitalism, post-growth, post-consumerism? Eco-political hopes beyond sustainability. Global Discourse, 7(1), pp.42-61.

18. Prahalad, C.K., 2012. Bottom of the Pyramid as a Source of Breakthrough Innovations. Journal of product innovation management, 29(1).

19. Friedman, T., 2005. The world is flat. New York: Farrar, Straus and Giroux, 488.

20. Krugman, P., 1994. The fall and rise of development economics. Rethinking the development experience: Essays provoked by the work of Albert O. Hirschman, pp.39-58.

21. Brown, S.L. and Eisenhardt, K.M., 1998. Competing on the edge: Strategy as structured chaos. Harvard Business Press.

22. Polanyi, K. and MacIver, R.M., 1944. The great transformation (Vol. 2, p. 145). Boston: Beacon press.

23. Chaffin, J. (2020). Can New York avoid a coronavirus exodus? | Free to read. [online] ft.com. Available at: ft.com/content/a313a40c-b046-4b11-b302-41d9f347cddb [Accessed 31 Jul. 2021].

24. etymonline.com. (n.d.). talent | Origin and meaning of talent by Online Etymology Dictionary. [online] Available at: etymonline.com/word/talent [Accessed 31 Jul. 2021].

25. britannica.com/topic/Transylvanian-Saxons

26. theguardian.com/commentisfree/2009/oct/01/romania-saxon-conservation-village

27. novinky.cz/historie/clanek/historik-martin-wihoda-o-pocatcich-ceskych-dejin-za-vzestupem-stalo-krestanstvi-i-otrokarstvi-40333819

28. Weber, M. and Kalberg, S., 2013. The Protestant ethic and the spirit of capitalism. Routledge.

29. Oxford Reference. (n.d.). Encyclopédie. [online] Available at: oxfordreference.com/view/10.1093/oi/authority.20110803095750863 [Accessed 1 May 2021].

30. Graham, L.R., 1992. Big science in the last years of the big Soviet Union. Osiris, 7, pp.49-71.

31. Wikipedia Contributors (2019). Valentina Tereshkova. [online] Wikipedia. Available at: en.wikipedia.org/wiki/Valentina_Tereshkova [Accessed 20 Oct. 2021].

32. Chambers, E.G., Foulon, M., Handfield-Jones, H., Hankin, S.M. and Michaels, E.G., 1998. The war for talent. McKinsey Quarterly, pp.44-57.

33. Hourani, A., 2013 [1991]. A history of the Arab peoples: Updated edition. Faber & Faber.

34. Wallace-Hadrill, A., 2017. Imperial Rome: a city of immigrants?. Acta ad archaeologiam et artium historiam pertinentia, 29, pp.53-72.

35. UNESCO (2021). Danube Limes added to UNESCO's World Heritage List closing this year's inscriptions. [online] UNESCO. Available at: en.unesco.org/news/danube-limes-added-unescos-world-heritage-list-closing-years-inscriptions [Accessed 31 Jul. 2021].

36. Deleuze, G., 2004. Anti-Oedipus. A&C Black.

37. Lasi, H., Fettke, P., Kemper, H.G., Feld, T. and Hoffmann, M., 2014. Industry 4.0. Business & information systems engineering, 6(4), pp.239-242.

38. Edmondson, A.C., 2018. The fearless organization: Creating psychological safety in the workplace for learning, innovation, and growth. John Wiley & Sons.

39.   Perry, M.J. (2019). Only 52 US companies have been on the Fortune 500 since 1955, thanks to the creative destruction that fuels economic prosperity | American Enterprise Institute - AEI %. [online] American Enterprise Institute - AEI. Available at: aei.org/carpe-diem/only-52-us-companies-have-been-on-the-fortune-500-since-1955-thanks-to-the-creative-destruction-that-fuels-economic-prosperity [Accessed 31 Jul. 2021].

Chapter 3 — The decade's new currencies: data, talent, learning

1.   mathscareers.org.uk/the-rice-and-chessboard-legend

2.   hostingtribunal.com/blog/big-data-stats/#gref

3.   IDC Media Center (2020). IDC's Global DataSphere Forecast Shows Continued Steady Growth in the Creation and Consumption of Data. [online] IDC.com. Available at: idc.com/getdoc.jsp?containerId=prUS46286020 [Accessed 31 Jul. 2021].

4.   Gantz, J. and Reinsel, D., 2011. Extracting value from chaos. IDC iview, 1142(2011), pp.1-12.

5.   Klein, M.C. (2020). Moore's Law Is Ending. Here's What That Means for Investors and the Economy. [online] Barron's. Available at: barrons.com/articles/moores-law-is-ending-heres-what-that-means-for-investors-and-the-economy-51605297625 [Accessed 10 May 2021].

6.   Shankland, S. (2020). Intel shows how it'll keep Moore's Law ticking so your 2025 laptop won't suck. [online] CNET. Available at: cnet.com/news/how-intel-will-keep-moores-law-cranking-for-years-to-come [Accessed 13 Feb. 2021].

7. Hale, J. (2019). More Than 500 Hours Of Content Are Now Being Uploaded To YouTube Every Minute - Tubefilter. [online] Tubefilter. Available at: tubefilter.com/2019/05/07/number-hours-video-uploaded-to-youtube-per-minute [Accessed 11 Nov. 2020].

8. Lin, Y. (2021). Top 10 WhatsApp Statistics You Should Know in 2021. [online] Oberlo. Available at: oberlo.ca/blog/whatsapp-statistics [Accessed 15 Apr. 2021].

9. IDC Data Age 2025. The Digitization of the World.

10. IDC Media Center (2020). IDC's Global DataSphere Forecast Shows Continued Steady Growth in the Creation and Consumption of Data. [online] IDC.com. Available at: idc.com/getdoc.jsp?containerId=prUS46286020 [Accessed 31 Jul. 2021].

11. Vollenweider, M., 2016. Mind+ Machine: A Decision Model for Optimizing and Implementing Analytics. John Wiley & Sons.

12. Maughan, T. (2020). The Modern World Has Finally Become Too Complex for Any of Us to Understand. [online] Medium. Available at: onezero.medium.com/the-modern-world-has-finally-become-too-complex-for-any-of-us-to-understand-1a0b46fbc292 [Accessed 5 Dec. 2020].

13. Korzeniowski, P. (2015). Big Data And ROI: An Uneasy Pairing For CIOs. [online] InformationWeek. Available at: informationweek.com/big-data/big-data-analytics/big-data-and-roi-an-uneasy-pairing-for-cios/a/d-id/1322050#:~:text=Big%20Data [Accessed 10 Jan. 2021].

14. Bradley, J., Loucks, J., Macaulay, J., Noronha, A. and Wade, M., 2015. Digital vortex: How digital disruption is redefining industries. Global Center for Digital Business Transformation: An IMD and Cisco initiative, pp.6-16.

15. Gothelf, J., 2014. Bring agile to the whole organization. Harvard Business Review, 92(11).

16. SCB & IMD ACCELERATING DIGITAL TRANSFORMATION AT THAILAND'S OLDEST BANK. (2019). [online] EFMD. efmdglobal. org/wp-content/uploads/SCB-IMD-EiP2019-FullCase.pdf [Accessed 31 Jul. 2021].

17. Banchongduang, S. (2021). SCB eager to usher in digital transformation. Bangkok Post. [online] 4 Jun. bangkokpost. com/business/2126667/scb-eager-to-usher-in-digital-transformation [Accessed 30 Jun. 2021].

18. AmericanHistory.SI.edu. (2019). Lighting A Revolution: 19th Century Consequences. [online] Available at: americanhistory. si.edu/lighting/19thcent/consq19.htm [Accessed 12 Dec. 2020].

19. Platt, H.A. (n.d.). Gas and Electricity. [online] Encyclopedia of Chicago. Available at: encyclopedia.chicagohistory.org/ pages/504.html#:~:text=The%20arrival%20of%20Samuel%20 Insull [Accessed 7 May 2021].

20. Brown, R.J., 2004. Manipulating the Ether: The power of broadcast radio in thirties America. McFarland.

21. Verger, J.D., 2012. Melding Fiction and Reality in HBO's Carnivàle. TV/Series, (1).

22. Chakravorti, B. and Chaturvedi, R.S., 2017. Digital planet 2017: How competitiveness and trust in digital economies vary across the world. The Fletcher School, Tufts University, 70, p.70.

23. Soper, T. (2017). Starbucks teams up with Ford and Amazon to allow in-car orders via Alexa. [online] GeekWire. Available at: geekwire.com/2017/starbucks-partners-ford-amazon-allow-car-orders-via-alexa [Accessed 10 Aug. 2020].

24. Brynjolfsson, E., Hu, Y.J. and Smith, M.D., 2006. From niches to riches: Anatomy of the long tail. Sloan management review, 47(4), pp.67-71.

25. Charan, R., n.d. The New Corporation: Reimagining Organizations In The Age Of Amazon. [online] Corporate Board Member. Available at: boardmember.com/corporation-reimagining-organizations-age-amazon [Accessed 22 August 2020].

26. Mixson, E. (2020). AI, Data and Predictive Analytics: A look into Nike's Formula for Growth. [online] AI, Data & Analytics Network. aidataanalytics.network/business-analytics/articles/ai-data-and-predictive-analytics-a-look-into-nikes-formula-for-growth [Accessed 27 Nov. 2020].

27. Mena-Yedra, R., Gavaldà, R. and Casas, J., 2017. Adarules: Learning rules for real-time road-traffic prediction. Transportation Research Procedia, 27, pp.11-18.

28. Sargent, J. (2019). Report: Organizations are struggling to perform business analytics on growing data volumes. [online] SD Times. sdtimes.com/data/report-organizations-are-struggling-to-perform-business-analytics-on-growing-data-volumes/#:~:text=According%20to%20the%20survey%2C%20data [Accessed 1 Aug. 2021].

29. Zhang, R. (2018). Why Haier Is Reorganizing Itself around the Internet of Things. [online] strategy+business. Available at: strategy-business.com/article/Why-Haier-Is-Reorganizing-Itself-around-the-Internet-of-Things [Accessed 15 Nov. 2020].

30. Frost, P.J., 1999. Why compassion counts!. Journal of Management Inquiry, 8(2), pp.127-133.

31. According to OECD data for 2019, in France 20.5% of males aged 20-24 were reported as NEET, i.e., neither studying nor working. Worldwide, 34% of young women can be described as NEET. In South Asia, this figure goes up to 53%. Youth who are NEET are generally considered to be at risk of becoming socially excluded – individuals with income below the poverty-line and lacking the skills to improve their economic situation: OECD. (2019). Youth and the labour market - Youth not in employment, education or training (NEET) - OECD Data. [online] Available at: data.oecd.org/youthinac/youth-not-in-employment-education-or-training-neet.htm [Accessed 6 May 2021].ILO. (2017). Where do the world's NEETs live? [online] Available at: ilo.org/global/about-the-ilo/multimedia/maps-and-charts/enhanced/WCMS_598674/lang--en/index.htm [Accessed 25 Jul. 2021].

32. Duszyński, M. (2019). Gig Economy: Definition, Statistics & Trends [2021 Update]. [online] zety. Available at: zety.com/blog/gig-economy-statistics?gclid=Cj0KCQiA5bz-BRD-ARIsAB jT4ngxFfEyXiqVtI0q8NSOsnTGOhEcAotHAIAYqUwWZ1E6I4E3uI MbOb0aAsOQEALw_wcB [Accessed 26 Jul. 2021].

33. INs AND OUTs OF THE GIG ECONOMY. (2018). [online] PYMTNS. Available at: securecdn.pymnts.com/wp-content/uploads/2019/07/Gig-Economy-Index-August-2018-min.pdf [Accessed 31 Jul. 2021].

34. Ehrenreich, B., 2010. Nickel and dimed: On (not) getting by in America. Metropolitan Books.

Chapter 4 — Overcoming fears

1. Kolko, J., 2000. The death of cities? The death of distance? Evidence from the geography of commercial Internet usage. The internet upheaval: Raising questions, seeking answers in communications policy, pp.73-98.

2. Pinchot, G. and Pinchot, E., 1994. The end of bureaucracy & the rise of the intelligent organization. Berrett-Koehler Publishers, Inc., 155 Montgomery Street, San Francisco, CA 94104-4109.

3. Hamel, G. and Zanini, M., 2018. The end of bureaucracy. Harvard Business Review, 96(6), pp.50-59.

4. Mankins, M., 2014. This weekly meeting took up 300,000 hours a year. Harvard Business Review, 29.

5. Girod, S.J. and Králik, M. (2021). How organizations can design for agility and embrace uncertainty. [online] strategy+business. Available at: strategy-business.com/article/How-organizations-can-design-for-agility-and-embrace-uncertainty [Accessed 10 Jun. 2021].

6. Glaveski, S., 2019. Where Companies Go Wrong with Learning and Development. Luettavissa: hbr.org/2019/10/where-companies-go-wrong-with-learning-and-development Luettu, 6, p.2020.

7. Fromherz, A.J., 2011. Ibn Khaldun. Edinburgh University Press.

8. Weinberg, G.M., 1975. An introduction to general systems thinking (Vol. 304). New York: Wiley.

9. Cossin, D. and Hwee, O.B., 2016. Inspiring stewardship. Chichester: Wiley.

10. Tabuchi, H. (2013, September 17). Eiji Toyoda, promoter of the Toyota Way and engineer of its growth, dies at 100. The New York Times. Retrieved from nytimes.com/2013/09/18/business/global/ eiji-toyoda-promoter-of-toyota-way-dies-at-100.html?_r=1

11. Miller, J. (2013, September 20). Blogging for Lean disambiguation & true kaizen | Gemba Panta Rei. Retrieved from gembapantarei.com/2013/09/the_man_who_saved_kaizen.html

12. Ferguson, R.B., 2013. The big deal about a big data culture (and innovation). MIT Sloan Management Review, 54(2), p.1.

13. Ben-Hur, S. and Kinley, N., 2016. Intrinsic motivation: The missing piece in changing employee behaviour. Perspectives for Managers, (192), p.1.

14. Scott, K., 2019. Radical Candor: Fully Revised & Updated Edition: Be a Kick-Ass Boss Without Losing Your Humanity. St. Martin's Press.

15. Hemerling, J., Kilmann, J. and Matthews, D. (2018) 'The Head, Heart, and Hands of Transformation', BCG.com – Publications, BCG.com. Available at: bcg.com/publications/2018/head-heart-hands-transformation. (Accessed 1 October 2020)

16. Cossin, D. and Hwee, O.B., 2016. Inspiring stewardship. Chichester: Wiley.

17. Workforce Partnership Staff (2019). How Do Gen Z Employees Learn? [online] snhu.edu. Available at: snhu.edu/about-us/ newsroom/2019/04/gen-z-learning [Accessed 1 Aug. 2021].

18. Plaskoff, J., 2017. Employee experience: the new human resource management approach. Strategic HR Review.

19. nst.com.my/news/nation/2020/02/562309/more-and-more-graduates-are-facing-unemployment-malaysia

20. ozobot.com/blog/oz218-what-are-future-ready-skills-and-how-can-they-help-students-succeed

21. Alatas, S.H., 2000. Intellectual imperialism: Definition, traits, and problems. Asian Journal of Social Science, 28(1), pp.23-45.

22. Kraemer-Mbula, E., Tijssen, R., Wallace, M.L. and McClean, R., 2019. Transforming Research Excellence: New Ideas from the Global South (p. 296). African Minds.

23. Malik, C.H., 1982. A Christian critique of the university. Downers Grove, Illinois: InterVarsity Press.

24. D'Hombres, B., 2007. The impact of university reforms on dropout rates and students' status: Evidence from Italy. JRC Scientific and Technical Reports, 40507.

25. Ekathimerini (2020). University funding to be tied to metrics. [online] University World News. Available at: universityworldnews.com/post.php?story=20200711140900985 [Accessed 1 May 2021].

26. Jackson, D. and Bridgstock, R. (2019). Universities don't control the labour market: we shouldn't fund them like they do. [online] The Conversation. Available at: theconversation.com/universities-dont-control-the-labour-market-we-shouldnt-fund-them-like-they-do-124780 [Accessed 10 Jan. 2020].

27. universityworldnews.com/post.php?story=20160509235704472

28. bostonmagazine.com/news/2019/01/29/college-problem

29. Trow, M., 1973. Problems in the transition from elite to mass higher education.

30. Daugherty, P.R. and Wilson, H.J., 2018. Human+ machine: Reimagining work in the age of AI. Harvard Business Press.

Chapter 5 — The new landscapes, spaces and voices of talent innovation

1. Smith, W.K., Gonin, M. and Besharov, M.L., 2013. Managing social-business tensions: A review and research agenda for social enterprise. Business Ethics Quarterly, 23(3), pp.407-442.

2. Zahra, S.A. and Wright, M., 2016. Understanding the social role of entrepreneurship. Journal of Management Studies, 53(4), pp.610-629.

3. Young, J. (2018). How ClickDo grew from one freelance SEO consultant to a digital marketing agency. [online] The London Economic. Available at: thelondoneconomic.com/tech-auto/technology/how-clickdo-grew-from-one-freelance-seo-consultant-to-a-digital-marketing-agency/10/07 [Accessed 7 May 2021].

4. Bris, A., Cabolis, C. and Lanvin, B. eds., (2019). Sixteen shades of smart : how cities can shape their own future. Lausanne: IMD International.

5. Anderson, B., 2006 [1983]. Imagined communities: Reflections on the origin and spread of nationalism. Verso books.

6. Lanvin, B. and Lewin, A., 2006. The next frontier of E-government: Local governments may hold the keys to global competition. Global Information Technology Report, 2007, pp.51-63.

7. Townsend, A.M., 2001. Network cities and the global structure of the Internet. American behavioral scientist, 44(10), pp.1697-1716.

8. Shu, C. (2020). Ride-hailing was hit hard by Covid-19 — Grab's Russell Cohen on how the company adapted. [online] TechCrunch. Available at: techcrunch.com/2020/09/17/ride-hailing-was-hit-hard-by-covid-19-grabs-russell-cohen-on-how-the-company-adapted [Accessed 1 Aug. 2021].

9. Howell, P. (2020). Grab bolsters driver and delivery-partners' digital knowledge. [online] Singapore Business Review. Available at: sbr.com.sg/transport-logistics/news/grab-bolsters-driver-and-delivery-partners-digital-knowledge [Accessed 1 Jun. 2021].

10. Lanvin, B. and Lewin, A., 2006. The next frontier of E-government: Local governments may hold the keys to global competition. Global Information Technology Report, 2007, pp.51-63.

11. IMD Smart City Index

12. Prosperity & Inclusion City Seal & Award. (n.d.). What is Inclusive Prosperity? [online] Available at: picsaindex.com/what-is-inclusive-prosperity [Accessed 1 Aug. 2021].

13. Quoted from suitcaseentrepreneur.com

14. Hankewitz, S. (2020). Estonia to implement a digital nomad visa. [online] Estonian World. Available at: estonianworld.com/business/estonia-to-implement-a-digital-nomad-visa [Accessed 1 Aug. 2021].

15. The next garage. Silicon Valley in the pandemic. The Economist. 16 May 2020.

16. oecd.org/coronavirus/policy-responses/cities-policy-responses-fd1053ff

17. The Covid network. Phone data identify travel hubs at risk of a second wave of infections. The Economist. 16 May 2020.

18. IMD business school. (2019). IMD Smart City Index 2019. [online] Available at: imd.org/research-knowledge/reports/imd-smart-city-index-2019 [Accessed 1 Apr. 2021].

19. Sustainable Development Goals Partnerships Platform. (2012). Bilbao Ría 2000- Transformation of Bilbao, Spain through public/private partnerships - United Nations Partnerships for SDGs platform. [online] Available at: sustainabledevelopment.un.org/partnership/?p=2197 [Accessed 1 Apr. 2021].

20. Key messages of NRI 2020.

21. Eyvazova, G. (2020). Nobel Brothers' history in Azerbaijan. [online] GRATA International. Available at: gratanet.com/publications/nobel-brothers-history-in-azerbaijan [Accessed 4 Apr. 2021].

22. Visser, R. (2006). Histories of Political Imagining. Britain in Basra: Past Experiences and Current Challenges. [online] Historiae.org. Available at: historiae.org/cosmopolitanism.asp [Accessed 5 Apr. 2021].

Chapter 6 — Young values are the lifeblood of the new geographies of talent innovation

1. Frankl, V.E., 1985. Man's search for meaning. Simon and Schuster.

2. Nonaka, I., & Takeuchi, H. (2011, May). The big idea: The wise leader. HBR. Retrieved from hbr.org/2011/05/the-big-idea-the-wise-leader

3. Prossack, A. (2018). How To Make Your Workplace Millennial Friendly. [online] Forbes. Available at: forbes.com/sites/ashiraprossack1/2018/07/29/how-to-make-your-workplace-millennial-friendly/#71a0ef32409d [Accessed 1 May 2021].

4. Wootton, C. and Grundy, J., 2018. Millennials in the workplace. University Presentation Showcase Event. 25. encompass.eku.edu/swps/2018/graduate/25

5. Maslow, A., 1965. Self-actualization and beyond.

6. Higgs, M. and Lichtenstein, S., 2011. Is there a relationship between emotional intelligence and individual values? An exploratory study. Journal of General Management, 37(1), pp.65-79.

7. Martin, W. (2017). Study Finds Millennials Are Happier at Work Than Gen X-ers. [online] Inc.com. Available at: inc.com/business-insider/millennials-happiest-generation-at-work-robert-half-happiness-works.html [Accessed 1 Aug. 2021].

8. Greater Good. (n.d.). The Science of Happiness. [online] Available at: greatergood.berkeley.edu/podcasts/series/the_science_of_happiness.

9. Alatas, S.F., 2003. Academic dependency and the global division of labour in the social sciences. Current sociology, 51(6), pp.599-613.

10. Happify.com. (n.d.). The Science of Happiness - Happiness in Life | Happify. [online] Available at: happify.com/public/science-of-happiness/#:~:text=What%20is%20the%20Science%20of [Accessed 1 Aug. 2021].

11. Bachelard, G., 1971. The poetics of reverie: Childhood, language, and the cosmos (Vol. 375). Beacon Press.

12. nytimes.com/2019/03/21/business/rent-the-runway-unicorn.html

13. Henderson, J., 2020. How Singapore's DBS Bank Is Riding The Digital Innovation Wave. [online] CIO. Available at: cio.com/article/3539251/how-dbs-bank-is-riding-the-digital-innovation-wave.html [Accessed 22 August 2020].

14. hbr.org/2019/06/why-you-should-create-a-shadow-board-of-younger-employees

15. Jordan, J. and Sorell, M. (2019). Why You Should Create a 'Shadow Board' of Younger Employees. [online] Harvard Business Review. Available at: hbr.org/2019/06/why-you-should-create-a-shadow-board-of-younger-employees [Accessed 1 Jun. 2021].

16. Munzenrieder, K. (2017). Gucci's Secret to Success? A 'Shadow Committee' of Millennials. [online] W Magazine | Women's Fashion & Celebrity News. Available at: wmagazine.com/story/gucci-millennials-shadow-committee-alessandro-michele [Accessed 10 Jul. 2021].

17. LVMH. (n.d.). DARE - Initiative LVMH. [online] Available at: lvmh.com/group/lvmh-commitments/leadership-entrepreneurship/dare-initiative-lvmh [Accessed 1 Aug. 2021].

18. Gnaneswaran, D. (2020). The world's first-ever youth-led digital 'parliament' goes live with Microsoft Teams. [online] Microsoft Malaysia News Center. Available at: news.microsoft.com/en-my/2020/07/17/worlds-first-ever-youth-led-digital-parliament-goes-remote-with-microsoft-teams [Accessed 12 May 2021].

19. Cooperation and Development Network Eastern Europe. (2020). Outsmarting the paradigm [UPDATED]. [online] Available at: cdnee.org/outsmarting-the-paradigm-implementation-of-new-technologies-in-the-cities-updated [Accessed 1 Mar. 2021].

20. Ibid.

21. Carlopio, J. R., Andrewartha, G., & Armstrong, H. (2000). Developing management skills in Australia. Frenchs Forest, N.S.W: Pearson Education.

22. Buechel, B., Cordon, C. & Kralik, M. (2013) Indonesian Port Corporation: Entering the big league? IMD Case, IMD-7-1494.

23. Low, Y. (2020). Younger Singaporeans far more likely to support wildlife conservation than older ones: Survey. [online] TODAYonline. Available at: todayonline.com/singapore/younger-singaporeans-far-more-likely-support-wildlife-conservation-older-people-survey?cid=h3_referral_inarticlelinks_03092019_todayonline [Accessed 10 Mar. 2021].

24. Debord, G., 1992. The society of the spectacle. 1967. Paris: Les Éditions Gallimard.

25. TODAYonline. (2020). Gen Y Speaks: As first-time voters, this is what we look out for this GE. [online] Available at: todayonline.com/gen-y-speaks/gen-y-speaks-first-time-voters-what-we-look-out-ge [Accessed 15 Apr. 2021].

26. Reid, A. and Sehl, K. (2020). Genuine Social Media Activism: A Guide for Going Beyond the Hashtag. [online] Social Media Marketing & Management Dashboard. Available at: blog.hootsuite.com/social-media-activism [Accessed 1 Jun. 2021].

27. Low, Y. (2020). Younger Singaporeans far more likely to support wildlife conservation than older ones: Survey. [online] TODAYonline. Available at: todayonline.com/singapore/younger-singaporeans-far-more-likely-support-wildlife-conservation-older-people-survey?cid=h3_referral_inarticlelinks_03092019_todayonline [Accessed 10 Mar. 2021].

28. Mehlman, J., 1972. The 'floating signifier': from Lévi-Strauss to Lacan. Yale French Studies, pp.10-37.

29. EtymOnline.com. (n.d.). inspire | Search Online Etymology Dictionary. [online] Available at: etymonline.com/search?q=inspire [Accessed 3 May 2021].

30. Calvino, I., 1988. Six memos for the next millennium. Harvard University Press.

31. Musil, R., 2015. The Man Without Qualities: Picador Classic (Vol. 50). Pan Macmillan.

Chapter 7 — Revitalizing ambition and faith in the future

1. Bartlett, C.A. and Ghoshal, S., 1994. Changing the role of top management: Beyond strategy to purpose. Harvard Business Review, 72(6), pp.79-88.

2. Gartenberg, C., Prat, A. and Serafeim, G., 2019. Corporate purpose and financial performance. Organization Science.

3. Case, J. (2015). What is 'inclusive prosperity?' [online] People's World. Available at: peoplesworld.org/article/what-is-inclusive-prosperity [Accessed 12 Feb. 2021].

4. Ghoshal, S., 2005. Bad management theories are destroying good management practices. Academy of Management learning & education, 4(1), pp.75-91.

5. Ghoshal, S., Bartlett, C.A. and Moran, P., 1999. A new manifesto for management. MIT Sloan Management Review, 40(3), p.9.

6. Ghoshal, S., 2005. Sumantra Ghoshal on management: A force for good. Pearson Education.

7. Minoru Makihara, 75th AMP, 1977 - Alumni - Harvard Business School. (2004, January 1). Retrieved from alumni.hbs.edu/stories/Pages/story-bulletin.aspx?num=2014

8. Schumacher, E.F., 1978. Small is beautiful: economics as if people mattered. London: Blond & Briggs.

9.   Tidey, A. (2020). Millennials particularly disillusioned about democracy, report finds. [online] Euronews. Available at: euronews.com/2020/10/20/millennials-are-most-disillusioned-generation-about-democracy-report-finds [Accessed 15 May 2021].

10. Davies, W. (2018). Enlightenment Now by Steven Pinker review – life is getting better. [online] The Guardian. Available at: theguardian.com/books/2018/feb/14/enlightenment-now-steven-pinker-review [Accessed 1 Feb. 2021].

11. Minsky, H.P., 1994. Full employment and economic growth as objectives of economic policy: Some thoughts on the limits of capitalism.

12. Cohen, T., 2012. Telemorphosis: theory in the era of climate change, vol. 1 (Vol. 1). Open Humanities Press.

13. Meadows, D.H., Meadows, D.L., Randers, J. and Behrens, W.W., 1972. The limits to growth. New York, 102, p.27.

14. Meadows, D., Randers, J. and Meadows, D., 2004. Limits to growth: The 30-year update. Chelsea Green Publishing.

15. UN.org. (2018). Goal 10: Sustainable Development Knowledge Platform. [online] Available at: sustainabledevelopment.un.org/sdg10 [Accessed 1 Jun. 2021].

16. Stubbington, T. (2019). Global debt surges to highest level in peacetime. [online] Financial Times. Available at: ft.com/content/661f5c8a-dec9-11e9-9743-db5a370481bc [Accessed 13 May 2021].

17. UNU-WIDER. (2020). Press Release: Covid-19 fallout could push half a billion people into poverty in developing countries. [online] Available at: wider.unu.edu/news/press-release-covid-19-fallout-could-push-half-billion-people-poverty-developing-countries [Accessed 3 Jun. 2021].

18. Mwenda, M. (2021). Africa battles the coronavirus as it faces its first recession in 25 years. [online] LifeGate. Available at: lifegate.com/africa-coronavirus-economy-recession-debt [Accessed 5 May 2021].

19. UNESCO. (2020). Startling digital divides in distance learning emerge. [online] Available at: en.unesco.org/news/startling-digital-divides-distance-learning-emerge [Accessed 1 Jun. 2021].

20. Blühdorn, I., 2017. Post-capitalism, post-growth, post-consumerism? Eco-political hopes beyond sustainability. Global Discourse, 7(1), pp.42-61.

21. Willener, A. ed., 2013. The action-image of society on Cultural Politicization. Routledge.

22. Anderson, J. and Rainie, L. (2020). Conerns about democracy in the digital age. [online] Pew Research Center: Internet, Science & Tech. Available at: pewresearch.org/internet/2020/02/21/concerns-about-democracy-in-the-digital-age [Accessed 2 Jun. 2021].

23. Williams, S., 2020. Data Action: Using Data for Public Good. MIT Press.

24. Pinker, S., 2018. Enlightenment now: The case for reason, science, humanism, and progress. Penguin.

25. fig.net/resources/monthly_articles/2012/january_2012/4SurvsOfCaesar_2.pdf

26. plato.stanford.edu/entries/stoicism

27. dailystoic.com/what-is-stoicism-a-definition-3-stoic-exercises-to-get-you-started

28. Aurelius, M., 2013. Marcus Aurelius: Meditations, Books 1-6. Oxford University Press.

29. UNDP.Medium.com. (2020). Understanding digital nomads. [online] Available at: undp.medium.com/understanding-digital-nomads-38f71678e884 [Accessed 1 Jun. 2021].

30. Norbrook, N. (2020). Replay: 'In times of crisis dominant ideologies get challenged'- Piketty. [online] The Africa Report.com. Available at: theafricareport.com/38401/replay-in-times-of-crisis-dominant-ideologies-get-challenged-piketty [Accessed 1 Jun. 2021].

31. Kahloon, I. (2020). Thomas Piketty Goes Global. [online] The New Yorker. Available at: newyorker.com/magazine/2020/03/09/thomas-piketty-goes-global.

32. InclusiveBusiness.net. (n.d.). Using inclusive business to achieve the SDGs. [online] Available at: inclusivebusiness.net/IB-Universe/sustainable-development-goals [Accessed 1 Jul. 2021].

33. Sustainable Development Goals Fund (2018). From MDGs to SDGs. [online] Sustainable Development Goals Fund. Available at: sdgfund.org/mdgs-sdgs [Accessed 4 Jun. 2021].

34. Transitioning from the MDGs to the SDGs | United Nations Development Programme. (2016). [online] undp.org. UNDP. Available at: undp.org/content/undp/en/home/librarypage/sustainable-development-goals/transitioning-from-the-mdgs-to-the-sdgs.html [Accessed 1 Aug. 2021].

35. Sustainable Development Goals Fund (2018). From MDGs to SDGs. [online] Sustainable Development Goals Fund. Available at: sdgfund.org/mdgs-sdgs [Accessed 4 Jun. 2021].

Figures

Figure 1   Global Talent Competitiveness Index (GTCI)   33

Figure 2   Movement in the GII top 15, 2017-2021   35

Figure 3   Talent competitiveness over time   44

Figure 4   GTCI 2021: Cities Index   45

Figure 5   GTCI Scores versus GDP per capita   45

Figure 6   Network Readiness Index (NRI)   60

Figure 7   City e-Government vs Overall Network Readiness   107

Figure 8   Smart City Index 2021   118

Authors' Short Bios

Bruno Lanvin

Initially a mathematician and a specialist of international trade, Bruno Lanvin is a French economist who has lived in France, the United States, and Switzerland, and worked in over 70 countries. His research and publications have focused on information technology, innovation and talent strategies. He has over forty years experience in advising governments and large corporations, including 20 years at the United Nations and ten at the World Bank, where he held senior positions.

Since 2001, he has co-authored The Global Information Technology Report (NRI), the Global Innovation Index Report (GII), the Global Talent Competitiveness Index (GTCI), the Smart City Index Report, and the award-winning book 'Sixteen Shades of Smart'. Over the last decade, his research has focused on education and talent policies as a tool to accelerate growth. Through his responsibilities as a board member of various private and public organizations, he was able to heighten interest for education and talent strategies, and to promote the strategic formulation of knowledge strategies.

He holds a BA in Mathematics, an MBA (HEC), a PhD in Economics (Paris I-La Sorbonne), and is an alumnus of INSEAD (IDP-C) and MIT. Currently a Distinguished Fellow at INSEAD, he is both the President of IMD's Smart City Observatory, and a co-founder and director of Portulans Institute, a global thinktank that focuses on technology, innovation and talent. A father of four (and now a grandfather), he lives in Switzerland.

Osman Sultan

Born and raised in Beirut, Osman Sultan studied in Paris, where he received his engineering degree in 1983. He is also an INSEAD alumnus (IDP-C).

During his career, he received many international awards, including in 2018 ITP's Telecoms CEO of the Year, and has been recognized as one of the most influential business leaders in the Arab world. As the founding CEO of two of the most transformative telecoms operators in the MENA Region (Mobinil in Egypt in 1998 and Du in the UAE in 2005), Sultan set during his career several strategies translating the profound transformations that telecoms, the internet and digital worlds have been provoking in our lives.

Sultan fits the definition of a talent leader. He has been a member of the Global Talent Competitiveness Index's Advisory Board for several years. As a mentor in the telecoms sector, he is proud to have groomed more than 20 talented leaders who became CEOs of various operations across all continents. As the founder and chairman of Fikra Tech Advisory Services, he focuses on establishing the right platforms to allow the emergence of the new conversations needed between the technological, economical and societal dimensions of our common future.

Sultan is a father of five, and lives between the United Arab Emirates, Egypt and France.

Lightning Source UK Ltd.
Milton Keynes UK
UKHW050803120722
405696UK00002B/2

9 782940 485550